NEW DIRECTIONS FOR ADULT AND CONTINUING EDUCATION

Ralph G. Brockett, *University of Tennessee, Knoxville*
EDITOR-IN-CHIEF

Alan B. Knox, *University of Wisconsin, Madison*
CONSULTING EDITOR

W9-DCY-653

The Adult Educator as Consultant

Lois J. Zachary
Leadership Development Services,
Fayetteville, New York

Sally Vernon
National-Louis University, Chicago

EDITORS

Number 58, Summer 1993

JOSSEY-BASS PUBLISHERS
San Francisco

THE ADULT EDUCATOR AS CONSULTANT
Lois J. Zachary, Sally Vernon (eds.)
New Directions for Adult and Continuing Education, no. 58
Ralph G. Brockett, Editor-in-Chief
Alan B. Knox, Consulting Editor

LC 85-644750   ISSN 0195-2242   ISBN 1-55542-685-9

NEW DIRECTIONS FOR ADULT AND CONTINUING EDUCATION is part of The Jossey-Bass Higher and Adult Education Series and is published quarterly by Jossey-Bass Inc., Publishers, 350 Sansome Street, San Francisco, California 94104-1310 (publication number USPS 493-930). Second-class postage paid at San Francisco, California, and at additional mailing offices. POSTMASTER: Send address changes to New Directions for Adult and Continuing Education, Jossey-Bass Inc., Publishers, 350 Sansome Street, San Francisco, California 94104-1310.

SUBSCRIPTIONS for 1993 cost $45.00 for individuals and $60.00 for institutions, agencies, and libraries.

EDITORIAL CORRESPONDENCE should be sent to the Editor-in-Chief, Ralph G. Brockett, Dept. of Technological and Adult Education, University of Tennessee, 402 Claxton Addition, Knoxville, Tennessee 37996-3400.

Cover photograph by Wernher Krutein/PHOTOVAULT © 1990.

CONTENTS

EDITORS' NOTES

Continuous learning is essential to maintaining a competitive edge in the global marketplace. Organizations of all kinds are relying heavily on external consultants who understand how adults learn. Thus, in addition to traditional educational settings, adult educators are now responding to an increasing demand for their expertise from the realm of business and industry. "Being a consultant" has become a viable professional option as an area of adult education practice.

Little formal preparation exists for adult educators who want to establish themselves as consultants. Most adult educators back into the role and learn about what it means to be a consultant in actual practice. The information available on consulting focuses on the mechanics rather than the process of practice. In addition, as Amy D. Webb points out in this volume, far "too little is known about either the role or the personal characteristics of the consultant." The difficulties are compounded by the newness of the field: There is no precedent or defined professional area of practice and literature to which one can refer for guidance on that process.

This volume, *The Adult Educator as Consultant,* is a collection of personal reflections on consulting, written for the adult educator who is considering consulting as a form of adult education practice. The authors provide multiple perspectives of what it means to be an adult education consultant, insights into the process of consulting, and analysis of the practical and identity issues to be considered in setting up a consulting business.

The work of the consultant is described as an integral, credible, and viable area of professional practice for adult educators. Practical information is provided about building an adult education consultancy that is as continuously invigorating to the practitioner as it is to the clientele. Drawing on the experience of a dozen adult education consultants, this volume offers an overview of the multiple roles and professional opportunities available to the adult educator. Thus, it offers a potpourri of practice options and, within that potpourri, a diverse range of contexts and methods.

Some of the critical concerns facing adult education consultants include practical aspects of business planning, practice and product development, establishing a professional identity, marketing a consulting practice, creating networking opportunities, remaining current in the field, and continuously reinvigorating self and practice. This list suggests that a natural link exists between adult education practices and good consulting practices. The contributors here were selected because their practices exemplify that very point. Together, they represent practitioners across a broad spectrum of adult education settings, including organizations from both the nonprofit and for-profit sectors.

All of the contributors to this volume are consultants. Some are institutionally based, either as internal or external consultants. Some are full-time, others are part-time. They represent a diversity of backgrounds, affiliations, expertise, and knowledge and share the commitment to and primacy of practice grounded in sound principles of adult learning.

Stephen D. Brookfield explicitly interprets the process of consulting as an adult education process in Chapter One. He identifies four core adult education activities: encouraging self-directedness, honoring and analyzing experience, engaging in critical conversation, and fostering critical reflection.

In Chapter Two, Sally Vernon addresses various realities and options of practice. Shifting paradigms call for shifting strategies to overcome the problems of paradigm paralysis. Vernon describes some prevalent frustrations among practitioners as they attempt to deal with these changes.

Little is known about the role of or the person who is the consultant. In Chapter Three, Amy D. Webb, reflecting on findings from her own research, suggests how specific patterns of needs and values differentiate consultants from other professionals. Her findings raise important considerations for adult education consultants.

In Chapter Four, Lois J. Zachary reflects on entries in her "practice diary," covering typical concerns, issues, and activities that confront adult education consultants on a daily basis. Among these are the importance of establishing clarity on the roles and responsibilities of the consultant, the establishment of one's personal identity as a consultant, and the need for flexibility and creativity.

The tasks of developing and nurturing professional and personal relationships with others are among the most important in establishing and maintaining a viable consulting practice. They involve wise use of both human and technological resources. William A. Howe and William T. Vericker describe the ways in which adult learning consultants develop and nurture connections with colleagues and the various "customers" whom they serve. In Chapter Five, Howe takes the approach that adult education consultants, in order to thrive, must develop professional relationships with colleagues, know about available resources, and have a supportive network of family and friends. He outlines ways in which consultants can gain access to and maximize use of resources. In Chapter Six, Vericker details the role of technology in facilitating and nurturing the connections that are essential to the establishment and maintenance of a consulting practice.

Adult education consulting practices take many shapes and forms. For many practitioners, the primary question is "Which will it be—full-time or part-time consulting?" Norma S. Friedman, in Chapter Seven, and George B. Thomas, in Chapter Eight, offer two very different configurations of practice.

Each has multiple priorities, but their "home bases" and the operations are very different. Friedman discusses issues relevant to developing a consulting practice while employed in a full-time academic position and getting the best of both worlds. She examines how split work responsibilities can nurture professional passion and entrepreneurial spirit and, at the same time, connect with practice. Thomas, on the other hand, describes the current reality of a full-time consultant, a "soloist," who works in both the nonprofit and commercial worlds. His chapter reflects his evolution from contract researcher to consultant and his professional growth in that role.

Most adult educators would agree that they have a role as change agents. However, until recently, only a relatively small number would have openly claimed that role as a predominant component of practice. Whether assisting an individual, a group, or an institution, the adult educator who is an effective change agent is familiar with adult learning principles, has a well-grounded understanding of the collaborative learning process, and is knowledgeable about group facilitation skills. This foundation is essential in helping others prepare for, react to, adjust to, and benefit from change.

In Chapters Nine and Ten, two practitioners, Joan C. Goldberg and Gayle Moller, describe completely different learning environments in which they practice as change agents. For both, their primary consulting role is to facilitate change through group interaction in a climate of safety, trust, and credibility. Goldberg shows how her work with groups helps individuals to accept, cope, and grow with personal change. Moller describes how her work with groups promotes organizational change.

Building on Moller's context of organizational practice, Karen E. Watkins and Victoria J. Marsick, in Chapter Eleven, describe the process that must be undertaken to develop the learning organization. They define a learning organization, portray the role of the adult education consultant in facilitating paradigm shifts, and outline the dilemmas that adult educators can encounter as they guide the implementation of continuous learning strategies and the application of action technologies in organizational cultures.

In Chapter Twelve, we summarize the major themes of the prior chapters and recast them from the perspective of the joys, the frustrations, and the self-regenerating nature of the enterprise, which serves to reinvigorate both self and practice.

The Appendix, "Treasury of Tips, Traps, and Tidbits," is a practical amalgam of wisdom gathered from the volume's authors. It is presented as a resource for the aspiring, practicing, and reflecting professional.

The multiple perspectives presented are a sampler of many of the practice issues and concerns that adult educators may experience in establishing viable consulting practices. Our aim, to paraphrase Daloz (1986), is to indicate the landmarks, point out the dangers, and suggest possible routes and destinations, but we leave the walking to the reader.

Lois J. Zachary
Sally Vernon
Editors

Reference

Daloz, L. A. *Effective Teaching and Mentoring: Realizing the Transformational Power of Adult Learning Experiences.* San Francisco: Jossey-Bass, 1986.

LOIS J. ZACHARY is an education consultant with a private consulting practice in Fayetteville, New York.

SALLY VERNON is faculty chair and program director of the Department of Adult and Continuing Education, National-Louis University, Chicago, and is president of her own adult learning consulting firm.

Being a consultant should be understood as a process grounded in adult education.

Understanding Consulting as an Adult Education Process

Stephen D. Brookfield

Opening Scene: What Is Wrong with This Picture?

A wet Tuesday afternoon in November and we are on the outskirts of a medium-size town in the United States. The camera pans along a row of fast-food joints, warehouse outlets, and multiplex cinemas before zooming in on a midprice chain hotel. We track into the hotel lobby, where four people are grouped around a table littered with styrofoam coffee cups, half-eaten Danish pastries, and slips of paper headed with the legend "Critical Thinking Task Force." As the camera moves in closer, we eavesdrop on their conversation and quickly realize that three of the four are colleagues at a local organization. The fourth is a consultant, who is being scrutinized by the other three and who seems eager to obtain work as a consultant. One of the three is speaking to the consultant. "What we want," he is saying, "is a program that can get our people thinking critically. We know you're the expert on this so we want you to do a two-day workshop." "No problem," replies the consultant, "I can do that." Now the second of the three is speaking: "Ever since the CEO [chief executive officer] decided to change the culture at our place, we've been looking for someone to put our programs into effect." She looks straight at the consultant: "You're the expert on this, we're paying you to tell us how to do it. We don't want a lot of this 'touchy-feely' mush, we just want you to tell us what we need to know." "Oh, and by the way," chips in the third member, "we need your plan by next week, okay?" "No problem," replies the consultant, "a two-day workshop should be fine."

This hypothetical (but typical) scene resembles one of those "Find the Eight Mistakes in This Picture" magazine games that my children like. On the surface, things seem fine. A group of people work for an organization that wants a consultant to come in and do a specific job that the consultant feels is well within his or her capacity. There seems to be a meeting of the minds and a feeling among all involved that the consultant is working responsively for the organization's good. This picture of a congenial person meeting the organization's needs would, for some, capture the quintessential adult education approach to consulting. However, scrutinizing this scene from the perspective of adult education's conceptual foundations, we can see that there is indeed "something wrong with this picture."

First, the task being addressed has been identified from above. Where are the employees' voices here? The CEO seems to have decided to change the organizational culture by fiat. The problem faced by the consultant does not arise explicitly from learners' situations and has not been identified by them as important. Nor does there seem to be an attempt to build connections between what the CEO wants employees to learn and their own crises and dilemmas.

Second, the format of the activity has been determined in apparent disregard of the employees' own inclinations, levels of readiness, past experiences, or current motivations. The implication is that the consultant has the requisite expertise in the area of critical thinking, which will be displayed before people who will see its self-evident desirability. The consultant becomes little more than a cognitive peddler. All involved seem to ignore the possibility that there may be people within the organization who have considerable experience of this process and who could serve as cofacilitators and valuable resources. The educational need (critical thinking) and the format designed to address this need (two-day workshop) are predetermined and preprogrammed. Conversation among managers, workers, and consultant about the desirability of this need and about the appropriateness of the format involved is missing.

Third, there seems to be a complete lack of knowledge about what the process of developing critical thinking involves. Task and format are unproblematized. There is no attempt to scrutinize the assumptions underlying what critical thinking is and why it should be developed. Nobody is asking, "In whose interest is it that this will be done?" or "Whose needs are being met here?" The task is presented as self-justifying, its legitimacy derived solely from ascribed authority. No one has raised the question of how democratic values are being realized or crushed by this initiative. No one is considering how doing this makes the world a fairer, more compassionate place. In summary, what is missing from this picture are the four processes that define adult education: (1) trusting adults to control what and how they are learning and to act as self-directed learners, (2) ensuring that adults' experiences are honored and that these experiences are analyzed critically, (3) engaging in critical conversation among learners and educators, and (4) developing critical reflection through the assumptions clarified, the alternative interpretations drawn, and the repressive features unmasked. Taken together, these four adult education processes represent a struggle for agency: a struggle to understand one's own self and how that self is inescapably framed by, and interdependent with, social forces. They also represent a struggle to change or affect these elements of agency.

People engaged in this struggle are in a critical process that cannot be reduced to the kinds of neat formulas and unquestioned practices implied in the opening vignette. In this chapter, I outline the four processes that are axiomatic to adult education practice, and I suggest ways in which consultants can act in accordance with the spirit of these processes.

Treating People as Adults: An Adult Education Interpretation of Consulting

In casting adult education—and an adult education approach to consulting—as a struggle for agency, I am acting out of insights drawn from the traditions and practices of adult education. An adult education approach to consulting views people as sculptors of their own practices. It is an approach that refuses to talk down to people by implying that their lives were unsatisfactory and unreflective up to the magic moment when they had the good fortune to fall under the influence of a Svengali, an omniscient, critically reflective adult educator.

"Treating people as adults" is a deceptively simple phrase, rich in implications for consultants. It implies that those of us who assume the role of consultant are partners in development with our clients. An adult education approach to consulting does not set up an artificial division between consultants as completed, static, fully rounded entities and clients as unformed clay, waiting to be sculpted into smoothly finished and efficient units of production. Instead, consultants take the same risks in educational activities as do their clients, and they do this first and in the open. They offer their own private experiences for public scrutiny. They try to take different perspectives on their habitual actions and enlist the help of others in uncovering the unacknowledged personal, pedagogical, and political assumptions that underlie their practices.

Encouraging Self-Directedness. Of the four ideas that I suggest should frame how we act as consultants, self-direction has been open to the widest interpretation. It has been claimed to fit squarely into the tradition of emancipatory adult education because of its link to the process of empowerment (Hammond and Collins, 1991). Self-direction emphasizes the centrality of people creating and crafting their own educational destinies in the face of uniform, centrally imposed, oppressive options. It rejects the idea that people only develop when adult educators or consultants arrange educational opportunities for them. It acknowledges the need for adults to feel that at some basic level they are responsible for choosing the direction and form of their own development. This idea that people are agents of their own development has been expressed passionately in Horton's (1990) observations that as educators "what we do involves trusting people and believing in their ability to think for themselves" (p. 157) and that "if you want to have the students control the whole process, as far as you can get them to control it, then you can never, at any point, take it out of their hands" (p. 136).

Self-direction does not imply that we throw out all formally organized adult education efforts because they have not been planned and conducted by learners. It does mean, however, that educational efforts should be grounded explicitly, as much as possible, in people's own expressions of the crises and concerns that affect their morale, self-confidence, and social safety. The kinds of choices that adults make about the foci and forms of their own learning and development say a great deal about the qualities of their lives. Adults can be seen realizing their potential in making self-directed, well-informed choices from a range of possibilities. One of these choices could be to place themselves, for a time, under the external direction of an expert, a mentor, or a role model—in effect, to surrender their own external sense of self-direction. Provided this choice is freely made on the basis of the fullest information possible, and is not forced or coerced, it is entirely consistent to see this as an act of self-directed learning. The key points are that there is no concealment of significant information, that learners have access to the widest range of alternative activities and options, and that in their individual decision to seek external help they retain an internal sense of confidence in how this decision was made and how it fits into their overall development.

Honoring and Critically Exploring Adults' Experiences. One of the earliest writers on adult education described it as "a cooperative venture in non-authoritarian, informal learning the chief purpose of which is to discover the meaning of experience; a quest of the mind which digs down to the roots of the preconceptions which formulate our conduct" (Lindeman, 1925, p. 3). More recently, the concept of experiential learning (Boud, Cohen, and Walker, 1993) has exercised a powerful hold on adult educators' imaginations as they strive to convince learners that their life histories are worth something. Honoring adults' experiences by making them the focus of serious study is a value proclaimed by most adult educators. Freire (Horton and Freire, 1990, p. 66) has argued that "we cannot educate if we don't start—and I said start, and stay—[at] the levels in which the people perceive themselves, their relationships with others and with reality, because this is precisely what makes their knowledge." What some advocates of this position miss, but what Freire believes is of equal importance, is the value of taking a critical perspective on our experiences, and studying them for their distortions. Similarly, Horton (1990, p. 152), in describing his work at the Highlander Folk School (now called the Highlander

Research and Education Center) in Tennessee, stressed his lifelong belief that "the best teachers of the poor and working people are the people themselves. They are the experts on their own experiences and problems." He also argued that "people know the basic answers to their problems, but they need to go further than that, and you can, by asking questions and getting them stimulated, coax them to move, in discussion, beyond their experience . . . and when you begin to expand the experience and share your own, people will ask each other questions" (p. 136). He also commented on the role of the facilitator: "There's no such thing as just being a coordinator or facilitator, as if you don't know anything. What the hell are you around for, if you don't know anything? Just get out of the way and let somebody have the space that knows something, believes something" (Horton and Freire, 1990, p. 154).

Engaging in Critical Conversation. Engaging in critical conversation has always been a prized adult education process. Eduard Lindeman viewed cooperative and critical analysis of experience through group discussion as the quintessential adult education event. Freire's work focused on culture circles, and Horton's emphasized workshops as the core of the Highlander process. More recently, Habermas's ideas of the ideal speech situation, communicative action, and intersubjective understanding have been interpreted as organizing ideals for adult education (Mezirow, 1990; Welton, 1991). Collins (1991, p. 12) has described the ideal speech situation as "a superlative pedagogic encounter," which is "an ideal, though conceivably achievable, group learning experience where participants put forward their own views on the problem at hand, listen carefully and respectfully to those of others, and seriously examine all relevantly identified information." Engaging in this kind of conversation, in Collins's view, leads to "inter-subjective understanding that comes from individuals being open to what others have to offer while, at the same time, being willing to present their own viewpoints for critical assessment" (p. 11). Finding and creating opportunities for people to engage in critical conversation with one another about their experiences as learners and educators is a realization of Habermas's ideas that should be at the heart of our work as consultants.

Encouragement of critical conversations within organizations is, for me, one of the most important ways in which consultants can exemplify adult education processes. Consultants can help create critical conversations that approach certain ideal conditions. Such conversations should strive for *diversity*. Diversity is seen when participants in critical conversation are drawn from different cultures, classes, and genders, take a variety of ideological perspectives on common experiences, and express their perceptions in different voices. Consultants can play a valuable role by working to broaden the ethnic, gender, and class spread of participants and the range of experiences, cultures, and priorities that their voices represent in conversations.

The condition of *respectfulness* should frame the conduct of those involved in critical conversation. Respectful conversation precludes attacks on another's person. More particularly, it means that belittling, silencing, or denigrating another's speech solely because of personal prejudice or dislike is alien to the spirit of critical conversation. The condition of being *fully informed* as a participant in critical conversation means that consultants should help learners gain access to all relevant information about events and choices in their lives. When it is obvious that certain organizational interests wish to keep information (for example, conditions of workplace safety or sexual harassment) in the hands of the few and out of the minds of the many, then this gives consultants a clear mandate. It also entails that they ensure that all relevant perspectives on an issue be made available, unless they contradict the condition of respectfulness.

The condition of conversational *openness* means that conversation by powerful participants to a predefined conclusion must be avoided. If there are evident power discrepancies in a conversational group whereby managers always end up determining the group's agenda, a way can be found to establish ground rules that keep their influence to a minimum (for example, alternating the role of silent recorder around the group so that for part of the time division heads and even CEOs are required to be silent). The condition of *attention to the problematic* ensures that critical conversation is focused on the task of understanding the problematic aspects of taken-for-granted ways of thinking and acting. This condition involves three interrelated processes: identification of our assumptions, exploration of alternative interpretations, and critical judgment of the interpretation.

The *reflectiveness* condition of critical conversation values silence as an integral part of any conversational dynamic. Interpretive processing, speculation, and reflective analysis are essential if people are to draw meaning from their experiences as a basis for informed action. Consultants facilitating critical conversations can take steps to ensure that periods of reflective silence are accepted as a normal and necessary element of people's deliberations. At the forefront of critical conversation is the analysis of *experience,* in particular the attempt to understand how individual experience is socially formed. There is an effort to elevate what participants might dismiss as anecdotal, idiosyncratic experience to the central focus of concern.

Connectedness as an emphasis of critical conversation values the linking of insights to action in the world and the analysis of action in the world. Critical conversations are crucibles for the kind of praxis—the continuous spiral of action, reflection on action, further action, further reflection on action, and so on—envisaged by Freire (1970). In a critical conversation, we seek to locate our private troubles in the context of public issues, while considering forms of collective action in different situations that might change individual histories. We then reflect on the appropriateness of these forms of action and on how we might learn from our experience as we reenter the domain of action.

The reunification between the personal and political, the individual and collective, is the focus of the condition of *communitarianism*. This condition urges participants in critical conversation to search for common elements in seemingly idiosyncratic experiences and to discover common interests as a basis for collective action. As Horton and Freire (1990) both attest, the practice of asking deceptively simple questions can be an extremely powerful way of drawing people's attention to what they have in common. In groups that have difficulty meeting the condition of diversity stressed earlier, asking the "obvious" deceptively naive question may be one of the most important tasks facing consultants who seek to develop critical conversations.

Becoming Critically Reflective. The development of critical reflection is probably the "idea of the decade" for many of the adult educators who have long been searching for a form and process of learning that could be characterized as distinctively adult. Evidence that adults are capable of this kind of learning can be found in developmental psychology, where a host of constructs such as embedded logic, dialectical thinking, reflective judgment, postformal reasoning, and epistemic cognition describe how adults come to think contextually and critically (Brookfield, 1991). Applied to workers in development, critical reflection describes how workers become aware of the assumptions that frame their habitual actions and ways of reasoning about practice, and how they research these assumptions to decide whether or not they are well grounded in reality.

Putting Ourselves into Practice

How can consultants exemplify the lofty values enshrined in the four core processes of adult education? Instead of just thinking in terms of grand strategies for structural change, we must also remember to model the four core adult education processes in what we do. Consulting can be thought of as "a way of being" (Rogers, 1980). We can strive for the balance of credibility and authenticity that engenders trust. We can do our best to model commitments to critical openness, frailty, and democratic values. We can do this by the way in which we enter the organizations and communities where we are working, the way in which we listen seriously to people's accounts of their dilemmas and frustrations, the way in which we ground our practices in terms that connect to people's experiences, and the way in which we make clear that there are certain moral visions and political projects that define our practices.

Rather than putting theory into practice, we should put *ourselves* into practice by making a determined attempt to research our own practices and to find out the symbolic readings of our actions made by those with whom we work. Instead of selling ourselves as omniscient content and process experts, we should make organizations aware of the resources that their own experiences represent. Instead of coming in with our own closed agendas for organizational change, we should find ways of encouraging workers to identify, articulate, and then work through their own dilemmas using their experiences and insights as a starting point.

In my own consulting work, I try to use a problem formulation exercise in which workers write brief private descriptions of the dilemmas that bother them and then come together to reach consensus on which of these dilemmas are most pressing. As a way of addressing these dilemmas, they begin by developing good practice audits that spring from an analysis of their own good and bad experiences of the dilemmas concerned. When I have left the organization, workers have a collaboratively determined list of projects to work on and a sense that their own experiences are a good place to start. If I give a keynote speech of some kind, or I find myself cast in the role of outside "expert," I try to ensure that my speech is preceded or followed by a panel of employees talking about critical events in their own experiences or about the contradictions, omissions, and discrepancies between my comments and their experiences. If I can arrange for both things to happen, then so much the better. By having stakeholders act as expert commentators and critical reactors to the pronouncements that I make as an outside expert, I am attempting to send a symbolic message about the importance of attending to people's own experiences.

When consultants take on a more proactive role, individuals find it difficult to stand outside of their comfortable perceptual frames and interpretive filters. When they need to reflect critically on their assumptions and actions, we should do this against the backdrop of the organization's culture. A case for change can only be made if learners understand and are shown how that change is in their own best long-term interest. When adult educators can make their consultancy efforts mirror the four core processes of adult education, their impact is considerable.

We can help people jump out of their habitual, unquestioned patterns of reasoning by asking the "stupid" questions ("What do you mean by success?" "What is learning?" "How do you know someone is teaching well?" "What do you think your most important goals are?") that individuals avoid for fear of looking naive or foolish. We can also raise contentious questions about organizational dynamics of power and control that those working inside the organization fear to voice because of the potential negative consequences. When they ask the undiscussable and politically fraught questions about whose interests are being served by an innovation, or whose problems are addressed by a new program, outside consultants stand to lose far less than regular employees. Of course, consultants risk the loss of return business, and threats to their livelihoods. But in the long run they increase the likelihood of gaining reputations as people who can focus on the real reasons why things are happening and what should be in place.

Consultants can also contribute a kind of craft wisdom concerning the rhythms and dynamics of adult learning, particularly with respect to the learning of critical reflection. Being aware of the resistance to critical reflection, we can alert people to how this might be confronted. Knowing the emotional accompaniments to critical reflection, we can suggest how these might be addressed by the organization. Finally, in our actions, we can exemplify the kind of critical pragmatism or critical responsiveness that represents the best elements of the adult education tradition. We can make it clear that we stand for something; that the four core adult education processes represent, for us, non-negotiable elements of who we are and how we practice.

References

Boud, D., Cohen, R., and Walker, D. (eds.). *Using Experience for Learning*. Milton Keynes, England: Open University Press, 1993.

Brookfield, S. D. "The Development of Critical Reflection in Adulthood." *New Education*, 1991, *13* (1), 39–48.

Collins, M. *Adult Education as Vocation: A Critical Role for the Adult Educator*. New York: Routledge & Kegan Paul, 1991.

Freire, P. *Pedagogy of the Oppressed*. New York: Continuum, 1970.

Hammond, M., and Collins, R. *Self-Directed Learning: Critical Practice*. New York: Nichols, 1991.

Horton, M. *The Long Haul*. New York: Doubleday, 1990.

Horton, M., and Freire, P. *We Make the Road by Walking: Conversations on Education and Social Change*. Philadelphia: Temple University Press, 1990.

Lindeman, E. C. "What Is Adult Education?" Unpublished manuscript, Lindeman Archives, Butler Library, Columbia University, 1925.

Mezirow, J. *Transformative Dimensions of Adult Learning*. San Francisco: Jossey-Bass, 1990.

Rogers, C. R. *A Way of Being*. Boston: Houghton Mifflin, 1980.

Welton, M. "Shaking the Foundation: The Critical Turn in Adult Education Theory." *Canadian Journal for the Study of Adult Education*, 1991, 5 (1–2), 21–42.

STEPHEN D. BROOKFIELD *is Distinguished Professor of Education at the University of Saint Thomas, St. Paul, Minnesota.*

*In times of continual change the adult education consultant is
confronted with challenges and frustrations. The causes and
remedies are described in this chapter.*

The Realities and Options of Practice

Sally Vernon

The practice options available to the adult education consultant in today's
market are rich, numerous, and expanding. In a rapidly changing economic, demographic, and social environment, continuous learning is
being touted as the major vehicle for maintaining a competitive edge
(Zuboff, 1987; Senge, 1990). As the realization that learning is the key to
success surfaces among virtually all segments of our society, increasing
numbers of people are grappling with the question of how to integrate
learning environments that are continuously responsive to change into
their lives, organizations, and communities.

The expertise of consultants who understand the ways in which adults
learn is thus a highly valued commodity. As a result of the growing
awareness of the importance and power of learning, adult educators are
being recruited by a diverse range of organizations to provide leadership
in the efforts to establish continuous learning environments. For-profit
and nonprofit institutions, large and small businesses, education entities,
government agencies, community-based organizations, professional associations, and foundations now constitute an abundant source of opportunities for adult education consultants.

The breadth and substance of these burgeoning consulting opportunities are tremendously appealing to adult educators. Not only are these
business opportunities but also opportunities to "make a difference" in our
society, culture, and economy. As consultants, adult educators can face the
challenge of being on the cutting edge of change. Another bonus is that
they can be recognized as experts with the knowledge and skills that are
critical in managing the societal transformation that is now occurring.

Given this scenario, one may think that adult education consultants

NEW DIRECTIONS FOR ADULT AND CONTINUING EDUCATION, no. 58, Summer 1993   © Jossey-Bass Publishers

"live happily ever after." However, that is not always the case. In many instances, these consultants experience significant discrepancies between their perceptions of the consulting role and those of their clients.

Perspective Discrepancies in Adult Education Consulting Practices

Much to the consternation of adult education consultants, the role that often is assigned to them is that of providing a quick fix, fixing the quick fix that did not work, or manipulating data to demonstrate that "the solution" to critical problems and change has been found (see Brookfield, this volume). Needless to say, this is not the role that the adult education consultant expected or would choose. It is, however, frequently the reality, regardless of the setting in which the consultant is working. Unfortunately, organizations often are either underprepared or unprepared to conceptualize or operationalize the process of continuous learning. These discrepancies in perception and practice serve as a significant source of frustration for the adult education consultant who anticipates providing a leadership role in the creation of continuous learning environments.

Many reasons are given for the discrepancies between, on the one hand, the acknowledged need for continuous learning and the recognition that the adult educator is the expert of choice to meet this need, and, on the other hand, the realities of the adult education consulting practice. One reason put forward is that there is insufficient top-level support for the continuous learning initiative; another is that there are insufficient human and material resources to support such an initiative; yet another is that the "workers" are not ready to be engaged in the process of continuous learning.

While each of these reasons is credible, the most notable reason for the discrepancies between expectations and realities is the absence of substantive individual and organizational paradigm shifts. These shifts are essential to the establishment of a continuous learning environment. Barker (1992, p. 32) has defined a paradigm as a "set of rules and regulations that does two things: (1) it establishes or defines boundaries; and (2) it tells you how to behave inside the boundaries to be successful."

Institutionalized paradigms typically are manifested in organizational charts, performance criteria, heroes, rites and rituals, and values (Deal and Kennedy, 1982). These indicators are very effective in providing individuals and organizations with guidelines for surviving and, ultimately, for thriving. However, in the present era of continuous change, the same paradigms that produced success and a competitive edge in the past have become barriers to a consideration of new ways of thinking, doing, and being. The rapid and dramatic changes of this era require us to rethink the ways in which we do business and the skills that are necessary to maintain our economic competitiveness (Carnevale, 1991), and to revisit not only what we have to know but how we go about learning it (Zuboff, 1987; Watkins and Marsick, in press). In other words, a shift in existing learning paradigms is required in order to meet the challenge of continuous change and continuous learning.

Barker (1992) has suggested that the process of paradigm shifts encompasses three stages. The first stage is the paradigm effect. The paradigm effect is the inability to see through the filter of one's established paradigm. As a result, individuals and organizations perpetuate boundaries and behaviors that may no longer be relevant. The second stage of shifting paradigms is the recognition and acknowledgment by individuals or organizations that a paradigm shift is necessary. However, they do not see alternatives and do not have a clear vision about "what to shift to," much less "how to do it." The third stage, the actual paradigm shift, marks the ability of individuals or organizations to identify and test new ideas, strategies, and measures of success.

Shifting the Learning Paradigm

The adult education consultant must recognize that he or she eventually will collide with shifting learning paradigms and that management of the process of shifting paradigms is a part of providing the leadership role that the consultant must assume. In addition, the consultant must understand that these learning paradigms have driven individuals or organizations consciously and unconsciously for long periods of time. Consequently, to be effective, the consultant must recognize and carefully assess the current stage of the paradigm shift encountered and develop a parallel intervention strategy.

The following specific paradigm shifts are now occurring in the realm of adult education. They are essential to the establishment of a continuous learning environment and are therefore a part of the process of adult education consulting. These shifts entail valuing of not only teaching but also learning, not only formal learning but also informal learning, not only a "rugged individualistic" approach to learning but also learning through communities of individuals that cross organizational boundaries, not only individual but also group and organizational learning, not only the product of learning but also the process of learning, and not only learning of a specific skill but also learning how to learn.

The challenge that faces the adult education consultant is to identify strategies that (1) maintain the business relationship between the consultant and the client, (2) establish a recognition and acceptance of the need for a learning environment, (3) facilitate the development of a sound product or process that can meet the long-term needs of the organization, and (4) provide the impetus for the organization to truly shift paradigms.

Role of the Adult Education Consultant in Shifting Learning Paradigms

Across very different organizations, workers at all levels are recognizing the need for changes in their ways of doing business and are feeling immense pressure to find solutions quickly to the problems that they are confronting. An organization that is experiencing the paradigm effect responds to this pressure by devising multiple "solutions" and trying them on. Unfortunately, if typical, the organization pursues this course without adequate preparation, much less effective research and evaluation strategies, that can provide sound indicators that indeed a solution to a particular problem has been found.

The role of the adult education consultant in the first stage of paradigm shifting is to help the individual and organization "see" the paradigm under which they are operating, consider alternative paradigms that will be useful to them, and frame these efforts using a learning model rather than a problem-solving model. In this way, the individuals involved automatically experience continuous learning as they develop a continuous learning model for the organization. It is critical that the adult education consultant provide frequent opportunities for workers to reflect on the consulting process so that each individual understands and experiences not only the product that emerges but also the process.

Individuals and organizations who have moved to the second stage of the paradigm shift process know that individual and organizational learning strategies are necessary if they are to survive in this era of change. These organizations have recognized that there are alternative paradigms to consider in solving organizational problems. In addition, they know that the learning strategies that they have used in the past require reexamination and that new ways of learning must be incorporated into the organizational learning plan.

The role of the adult education consultant in the second stage of paradigm shifting is to establish a learning environment in which the individual and the organization can examine why previous learning strategies are now ineffective. A structure must also be provided that enables the client to experience and explore new learning alternatives and to identify means for integrating effective learning strategies throughout the organization. Finally, the adult education consultant must facilitate the development of a process that ensures continuity in individual and organizational learning and in paradigm analysis and shifting, as necessary.

Individuals and organizations in the third stage of paradigm shifting are examining and adopting new strategies for continuous learning and the means for incorporating these strategies throughout the organization. They also are identifying benchmarks for evaluating their success with continuous learning and determining "red flags" that indicate when it is time to consider new paradigms or to enhance existing ones.

The role of the consultant in working with clients in the third stage of paradigm shifting is to develop a process that enables the individual and organization to examine the thoroughness of their investigation of alternative learning strategies. The consultant also must provide for sound research strategies and evaluation methodologies that indicate whether "solutions" to organizational problems have been found and effective processes for continuous learning have been established.

There is a tendency to assume that companies will agree that the assumptions underlying these adult education consulting strategies are appropriate and that they will participate fully in developing and experiencing sound learning activities. This assumption should not be made. The consultant must engage in a collaborative learning process with the client to ensure that commitment to and ownership of the consulting agreement and activities are continuously and mutually satisfactory. This process includes the establishment of a relationship with the client that leads to ongoing communication, assessment, negotiation, and trust (Block, 1982). It also includes the negotiation of a contract that is specific enough to encourage accountability but flexible enough to allow for necessary changes. Authenticity from both the adult education consultant and the client ensures that there are few surprises in how each conducts himself or herself personally and professionally. Finally, a feedback loop is needed to encourage both parties to see the effectiveness of the goals, process, and product of the agreement.

Conclusion

This chapter focuses on the perspective discrepancies that frequently exist between the adult education consultant and the client in an environment of rapid and continuous change. These discrepancies and the context of change are realities of an adult education consulting practice. In particular, the discussion of the perspective discrepancies centers on the shifts in learning paradigms that are necessary to develop continuous learning environments. The consulting process that results in shifting paradigms defines practice options for the adult education consultant and reflects the theme that undergirds the problem-posing, problem-solving, and information-sharing aspects of the chapter. This theme is that adult education consultants are most successful in dealing with these issues and creating continuous learning models if they practice and model a continuous learning process themselves.

References

Barker, J. *Future Edge: Discovering the New Paradigms of Success.* New York: Morrow, 1992.

Block, P. *The Flawless Consultant.* San Diego: University Associates, 1982.

Carnevale, A. P. *America and the New Economy: How New Competitive Standards Are Radically Changing American Workplaces.* San Francisco: Jossey-Bass, 1991.

Deal, T. E., and Kennedy, A. *Corporate Cultures: The Rites and Rituals of Corporate Life.* Reading, Mass.: Addison-Wesley, 1982.

Senge, P. M. *The Fifth Discipline: The Art and Practice of the Learning Organization.* New York: Doubleday, 1990.

Watkins, K. E., and Marsick, V. J. *Sculpting the Learning Organization.* San Francisco: Jossey-Bass, in press.

Zuboff, S. *In the Age of the Smart Machine.* New York: Basic Books, 1987.

SALLY VERNON is faculty chair and program director of the Department of Adult and Continuing Education, National-Louis University, Chicago, and is president of her own adult learning consulting firm.

*Personal and professional characteristics of consultants reflect the
inherent nature of their work.*

Consultants and Their Work: The Learning Dynamic

Amy D. Webb

Too little is known about either the role or the personal characteristics of
the consultant. Are there distinguishing characteristics of who does this
work? How are the personal characteristics of the consultant related to this
professional role and the satisfaction derived from this work? Is there an
opportunity for personal development as consultants help clients learn and
change?

In my search for answers to these questions, the literature on consulting offered little help. We know much more about what consultants *do* than
who they are. I found that who consultants are and how they do their work
are interrelated. In fact, just as a consultant is an agent for organizational
change, so too a consultant can be seen as an agent for his or her own
personal satisfaction and development within the role. Not only is there a
need for would-be consultants to accurately assess their patterns of needs
and values to see how congruent they are with a consulting career, but
having made the choice to consult, there is a need for continual assessment
of how personal patterns relate to what one learns from consulting experiences. As with their client organizations, consultants can succeed by first
preparing themselves with a basic framework for understanding learning
and change.

Building of a Consultancy Starts with Self

In addition to the pragmatics of managing a business, consultants need to
understand and develop the following four components of a consultancy:
First, *role orientation and self-assessment* lay the groundwork for consulting.

This component requires that a consultant understand the nature of the work and the dynamic between the person and the role. Second, *skill building* identifies the need to assess which generic consulting skills are needed and which content-specific skills the consultant wants to develop. The skills repertoire that a consultant develops will ultimately influence the kinds of work that he or she can tackle successfully. Third, *experiencing and reflecting* define the actions of selecting work experiences congruent with one's needs and skills and reflecting on how well the experiences and results are building a desired portfolio. And, fourth, *ongoing feedback and learning* involve evaluation of how well the consultant is keeping track of successes and mistakes and the critical lessons learned from each. Feedback, along with the ability to reflect on it, is vital to the success of consultants and shapes the direction of their practices.

Ultimately, each of the four components are linked in a kind of learning spiral rather than a linear track. Consultants address each component sequentially and simultaneously. Over time, the components are experienced again and again, but each time with higher levels of self-knowledge and consulting experience. The four components interact to produce patterns of development. The model suggests that personal patterns repeat and evolve as consultants connect themselves with their learning.

Although each component is important, the first component is critical to movement within the spiral. Attention to the role orientation and self-assessment component can make the difference between a successful and unsuccessful consulting practice. The remainder of this chapter elaborates on the orientation and assessment component and shows how it is linked to the other three components.

Nature of Consulting: The Role-in-Context

There are three basic contexts that consultants need to explore and understand in order to achieve congruence and satisfaction with their work. First, they need to understand the nature of the work, the role-in-context. This includes the characteristics of the consulting role, the needs and values that differentiate consultants from other professionals, and the relationship between type of practice and consultant characteristics. Next, they need to understand themselves as consultants, the self-in-role. This area includes how the predominant needs and values of an individual are expressed through consulting work and how these individual characteristics relate to the experiences wrought from and lessons learned through the role. The third area involves an understanding of the interaction between who one is and how one creates a satisfying consulting role.

In my research on consulting, I surveyed and interviewed a random sample of over two hundred consultants working full-time in the areas of management development and organizational change. My findings shed light on the vocation of consulting.

The interpretive framework of my research is based on Schein's concept of "career anchors." Schein (1975) classified the needs, values, and talents of organization managers into stable predictors of work satisfaction. These predictors, or anchors, are meaning structures for individuals, guiding what they seek and commit to in career experiences. Schein (1975, p. 11) described an anchor as "a combination of perceived areas of competence, motives and values that you would not give up; it represents your real self. Without knowledge of your anchor, outside incentives might tempt you into situations or jobs that subsequently are not satisfaction because you feel that 'this is not really me.' "

Expanding Schein's typology, I tested nine anchors: technical competence, managerial competence, autonomy, security, service, creativity, variety, impact, and influence. I determined how individual differences show up in the way in which consultants describe what is satisfying and troubling in their work.

Not only does the specific cluster of anchors for consultants characterize the needs of the majority of consultants studied, but it also fits the general descriptions on consulting written by theorists and practitioners. The work of consulting involves the application of technical expertise to help a client with a particular task. Autonomy is generally involved through the discretion afforded in assignments, schedules, and interventions. Autonomy is also realized as a result of the consultant's external position in relation to the client's problems. The consultant is thus free to independently analyze the problem and articulate the salient issues for the client. Finally, consulting is service. Consultants are engaged by organizations to provide help, to meet the needs that the organizations cannot meet alone.

Individual consultants may have one or more of the predominant anchors above, as well as any other anchors defined in Schein's (1975) typology. These anchors are manifested in how individuals perform the consultant role and what they describe as meaningful and satisfying experiences. Consultants claim a higher degree of career satisfaction than do managers, which may be due to their greater freedom to shape their work role in ways that directly satisfy personal development needs. Given that more consultants than managers have multiple dominant anchors, the context of the consulting role must be sufficiently broad and rich to enable these anchors to be fulfilled for any one consultant.

Consulting as a career produces high levels of growth and satisfaction as a function of what consultants collectively bring to the role in terms of career anchors, and how well their anchors map onto the design of the work. A composite perspective from consultants, representing the anchors, characterizes the consulting role as follows: complex issues and challenges (technical competence); freedom and control (autonomy); choices and variety in tasks, clients, people (variety); customer-oriented work, helping clients grow (service); making a difference, changes at high levels of the organization (impact); using oneself as an instrument of change (influence); and innovative approaches to problem solving (creativity).

When asked about the nature of consulting, consultants represented their anchors in their responses. One consultant, anchored in autonomy, described consulting's attraction as "the freedom to leave your unique mark on the work . . . freedom from organizational norms and politics . . . freedom to work anywhere." Another consultant, anchored in variety, said, "It is collecting knowledge from others and your own varied experiences and converting them to a credible and useful language for a client. . . . It is new interests and things to learn." Still another, anchored in service, claimed, "Work is my ministry. I help organizations commit to their values and act congruently. . . . I help people connect what they do and who they are. . . . I believe in them."

From these examples, one can see that consulting as a career role is attractive to those who have great need to express their value for technical competence, autonomy, and service, as well as a combination of other needs and values. However, in my study, most of the consultants worked for themselves as solo practitioners or with outside associates. It is noteworthy that the consultants who worked in consulting firms (a structured organization of three or more, typically more than ten) had significantly higher security anchor scores than the consultants who had their own practices. This result raises the question of how much work structure or organizational size is a factor in attracting consultants with particular anchors.

Another factor in matching personal needs with the role may be the particular content area of the consultant. My research indicated that consultants with particular configurations of anchors were likely to gravitate toward a particular practice area. For instance, the anchor profiles of management development consultants differed from those of Total Quality Management consultants. This suggests the need for future research to identify the profiles of consultants by type (for example, adult educators).

Nature of the Consultant: The Self-in-Role Context

The consulting role enables consultants to develop and experience growth. Consultants, by the nature of their needs and values, inform the role. Consulting, as a career role, offers a broad enough context to enable multiple anchors to be fulfilled. What is critical to consultants' satisfaction with the work is their own accurate assessments of self. Self-knowledge about what drives them in this work, each individual's unique combination of needs, values, and talents, is an essential first step toward congruent career choice and professional development.

The first part of the role orientation and self-assessment process highlights the need to understand the character of the consulting role. The next part asks a somewhat different question: "Which inherent facets of the individual seek expression or satisfaction through work, and what might that expression look like in a consulting role?" Essentially, my premise is that consulting offers an arena for personal development, but only insofar as a consultant is willing to ask what he or she is driven to learn through the work and what successes and mistakes are likely, given one's anchor structure.

With the assumption that individuals are the agents for their own work satisfaction, it is clear that consultants can and do use their role to develop themselves and find personal meaning. Theorists have described the more successful consultants as "instruments" of change—people who can be authentic, fully themselves, capable of reading the internal and external cues of a change process. To take the metaphor further, the self-as-instrument means knowledge about the kind of music that is natural for one to play, the tuning required to stay in key, and the kinds of pieces that require one to practice and stretch limits. If the instrument of the self is depicted in the patterns of one's needs and values (anchors), as I am suggesting, then those patterns should be discoverable, as are the distinct sound patterns of musical instruments. Evidence supports this idea. As I talked with over forty consultants and studied their words, I learned about the emphasis within different anchors. I began to hear the language that consultants use to describe what they do to create meaning through their work, and how what they learn is related to that larger meaning.

For example, one consultant, with autonomy and service as primary anchors, talked about her need to "stand on my own. . . . I'm always looking for more affiliations with clients, more relationships to build so I can have choices about saying yes and no." Still another consultant, driven by impact and influence needs, described how consulting provides "a sense of achievement and relationship. . . . I am the source of making a difference. . . . I have to keep stretching myself, looking to the next challenge, dealing with my fears, and letting go. . . . As I am clear about what I want and need, I put it out there, and it helps the client do the same."

Consultants anchored in service and variety discussed the way in which they do the work of consulting: "I look for alternative strategies to help people identify what they could do versus not do. . . . I have to think on my feet, field the emotions of the group. I ask questions, lots of them, to help people move. . . . I call on different viewpoints to focus the client."

Variety paired with creativity was revealing: "I find multiple ways of thinking about things. . . . I scheme about what's the craziest thing I can do to loosen up the group. . . . I read different things to find new things to try together with the client. We both learn." These examples provide at least initial indications of how different anchors are fulfilled through the consulting role, and how people with different anchors see and shape the role.

The value in self-assessment at the beginning of and throughout a consulting career lies in the potential for congruence between an individual and his or her work, as well as in the increased openness toward learning. Having established that there is a link between the nature of consulting work and the fact that what motivates an individual to pursue a consulting career affects how he or she sees and performs the work, I now turn to a discussion of how career anchors relate to what a consultant learns through work.

There is a strong connection between what an individual learns through consulting work and the needs and values that serve as anchors. The role provides the context wherein these factors connect. Specifically, a consultant's anchor pattern is related to what he or she is likely to experience as successes and mistakes, and to the developmental challenges within the role. There is convincing evidence that the inherent strengths of one's primary anchor or anchors relate to consulting successes, whereas the weaknesses or overapplied strengths relate to mistakes and development needs. Consultants experience situations within their work role that give them opportunities to deal with issues of their own development.

For example, consultants anchored in service described themselves as "emotionally drained holding the energy for the client group." They talked about accommodating clients to their own disadvantage, as in "feeling badly about taking a vacation." They spoke of their lack of family time and personal balance, and their loss of control: "I am always wrestling with being taken advantage of. . . . I want to give my time away more than I can afford to." The developmental issues for consultants with this anchor may be, among others, managing boundaries between themselves and their clients, not getting hooked by unrealistic expectations for change, not building dependency relationships with clients, and taking time for themselves.

Likewise, for consultants anchored in service, the patterns of successes and mistakes that they discussed were related to their needs and values. For example, these consultants reported successes that involved giving themselves to clients to create change: "I opened doors for them. . . . Because of my intense personal attention, the client began to manage itself like it should. . . . They told me I did them a great service."

The mistakes for consultants of this orientation were apparently also anchor-related: "I couldn't help them turn it around . . . too much was going on in the organization; I got caught in the same whirlpool. . . . I worked so hard with those in pain I failed to get higher-level support. . . . They needed crisp, logical analysis; I wasn't objective enough. . . . I didn't connect; I let things pass that needed confronting."

A challenge for adult educators is to be aware of how their career anchors play out in terms of their strengths and weaknesses. Knowledge about their own anchor patterns can help consultants see how best to utilize their strengths and learn to manage weaknesses as well as see when their strengths are becoming weaknesses.

Bellman (1990) discussed the paradoxical truth that major growth opportunities for consultants come in areas where they have already done well. Confidence in strengths can become overconfidence. Habits of success can blind them to overused strengths. Consultants may derail if they are not aware of how their personal orientations can bring on difficulties. The contribution of their anchor orientations protects their Achilles' heels. For example, a variety-anchored consultant reported these positive characteristics of his work orientation, and the corresponding liabilities: "I like to learn. . . . I'm always thinking how I can adapt, change directions, update materials, and stay flexible. . . . What I have trouble with is the 'bread-and-butter' work . . . the tenth running of a course. . . . I get bored." Another consultant with the same primary anchor reported, "I call on a variety of experiences and generate lots of alternatives, but I end up taking over the responsibility for change because the client has no ownership."

Finally, by analyzing the successes and mistakes that the consultants made, and extracting underlying strengths and weaknesses related to their anchors, I also found the paradoxes within each orientation that need to be managed. For the variety-anchored consultant, the paradoxes may be related to overcommitment: "The value of having a lot of clients and experiences is threatened by compromises of time with them to be able to fit them all in. . . . I get overcommitted to finding alternatives, and when the client begins to close down on options I get rigid about my way of keeping open. . . . I'm like a butterfly on an unopened flower."

Certainly, more investigation is needed to articulate the link between learning and career satisfaction within particular consultant orientations. It seems clear, however, that satisfaction comes as a by-product of self-discovery and self-enactment through the consulting role.

Nature of the Dynamic: Self and Role

When consultants are asked questions about what attracts them to the role, what they see as trade-offs, how they receive feedback and how their needs are met and not met, they talk about how their work enables them to develop, and how their needs, in turn, inform the role that they perform. Schein (1985) described this phenomenon as a reciprocal learning process, where the career anchor is a learned part of one's self-image. The learning process is a function of what the consultant brings to the work situation as well as of the opportunities and feedback provided through the work. Consultants find their work meaningful as they learn who they are through the role. The work environment, then, plays a part, as well as the individual's ability to balance the trade-offs.

One young consultant whom I interviewed, who works for a midsize consulting firm, described the thrill and the fear of consulting: "You've got to know that your survival is in your hands . . . you make it; no one else can make it for you . . . you have to believe it." Although the autonomy needs in that description are apparent, consultants with other anchors also acknowledged that satisfaction means knowing their needs and developing useful strategies for fulfilling them. They know which important needs can be met through work, and which can only be met elsewhere.

The career anchors of consultants relate to the attractions that they find in the work, the perceived trade-offs, and the role issues that they find difficult. In my study, consultants with autonomy anchors saw freedom and flexibility in the nature of the work. However, they also identified financial security and working with others as key trade-offs. Both of these trade-offs are essentially opposites of their primary anchor.

Issues and clients that were most troublesome for consultants can also be seen as anchor-related. One of the consultants anchored in autonomy stated, "I can say no but I don't. I don't have a boss, but in reality I have six. . . . I can do independence; it's partnership and teamwork that are tough." An interesting aspect of these remarks is that when the characteristics of the anchor are overplayed, or expressed ineffectively, they can fuel the intensity of the trade-off. For instance, the characteristic of independence, "doing what I want when I want," can underlie a lack of self-discipline. The freedom to "tell the client the truth" may weed out clients and threaten financial security, a key trade-off for the autonomy-driven consultant.

For consultants, then, an understanding of who they are and what the consulting role means for them is key to their satisfaction. The source of career satisfaction relates to the ability of individuals to enact their needs and values through their work. The source of their dissatisfaction also stems from who they are, who they are not, and how they balance these identity factors within the consulting role. Feedback on how well their orientations are enacted is a vital component of the personal learning and professional contribution possible through consulting.

Relating Orientation and Assessment to Other Steps

The importance of role orientation and self-assessment for a consultant cannot be overstated. As with the other three components on the consultant's learning spiral, this first element is always evolving. Throughout his or her career, a consultant repeatedly assesses personal motivations and how these relate to performance and satisfaction.

Consultants can inventory their skills using their anchors as guides. Once the basic content skills and understanding of consulting processes are mastered, reflection on the results of experiences can serve as an ongoing needs analysis. Reflection on what one does well and not so well, on what is particularly difficult about one's work processes and assignments, and on feedback from clients or co-workers is essential to learning about one's developmental needs.

The third and fourth components—experiencing/reflecting and ongoing feedback/learning—occur linearly, or, for more active and disciplined learners, simultaneously. The selection of those consulting experiences that fit with one's strengths, or that can enhance one's development, is an ongoing challenge for individual consultants as well as consulting organizations. It is often too easy to repeat what one does well without seeing the long-term developmental limitations of this strategy. Consulting assignments, if viewed by consultants as learning and development opportunities, challenge individuals to be mindful of what they are learning, how this relates to their personal needs and values, and what is likely needed for future strengthening of self in the consulting role.

At least after a consulting experience, if not during it, consultants can assess their successes and mistakes and see how these are related to their developmental needs within the framework of their anchor patterns. In this way, consultants can sharpen their skills in an informed and personally meaningful way and, with respect to future assignments, optimally contribute to their own and their client's well-being. There is no substitute for experience in the development of consulting skills, but whether their experience is viewed as repetitive or rich may directly affect the learning and satisfaction of consultants.

References

Bellman, G. M. *The Consultant's Calling: Bringing Who You Are to What You Do.* San Francisco: Jossey-Bass, 1990.

Schein, E. H. "How Career Anchors Hold Executives to Their Career Paths." *Personnel*, 1975, 52 (3), 11–24.

Schein, E. H. *Career Anchors: Discovering Your Real Values.* San Diego: University Associates, 1985.

AMY D. WEBB *is a principal consultant with Change Management, Inc., and serves on the adjunct staff of the Center for Creative Leadership, Greensboro, North Carolina.*

The author's reflections on personal diary entries describe everyday struggles, concerns, and issues that confront adult education consultants.

Choosing to Be a Consultant: This Is a Living?

Lois J. Zachary

I am a full-time adult education consultant. I chose this profession because it provides a living that is challenging, exciting, diverse, forever changing, and stimulating. When I first began working as an education consultant, however, I would frequently reexamine my nontraditional career choice and inwardly jest, "This is a living?" Today, I have no doubt that I chose wisely. As a consultant, I derive an enormous amount of personal and professional satisfaction from my work.

As adult learners are found in diverse settings, my "workplace" is ever-changing, as are the labels attached to and perceptions of what it is I "do." I am called a trainer, an education consultant, a staff developer, a process consultant, and a leadership and board development consultant. The nature of my practice brings me to diverse locations and into a variety of settings. Therefore, in any one month, it is not unusual for me to be "on the road," traveling to several sites. I might be delivering a keynote address, conducting a workshop, leading a retreat, working on a research project, meeting with current clients, preparing a report or article, or presenting a seminar. No two months are alike. In fact, changing clients and settings are the norm of my consulting practice.

In this chapter, I reflect on entries from my personal diary in order to recount the realities of my practice and to share insights into the competing demands that confront an adult education consultant on a daily basis. With the aid of one diary excerpt from each season of the year, I recall four days in my life that together paint an especially clear picture of the variegated landscape that frames my practice. The orderliness and structure of my workdays are as variable as the activities and multiple settings in which I practice. The specific work changes on a daily basis, but the issues and concerns that affect those activities transcend the day-to-day variations in my professional life.

Winter: A Snowy January Morning

Futurists such as Naisbitt (1982) began writing about the concept of the cottage industry well over a decade ago. Even though that was exactly how I was operating my business, I never connected the term *cottage industry* directly with my work, a private consulting practice specializing in adult development and learning as well as leadership development. My mental image of a cottage was linked to fairy tales—specifically, where Snow White lived with the Seven Dwarfs. It is a different kind of "snow white," however, that captures the image and convinces me that my consulting business, situated in an office in my home, is truly a cottage industry:

It is a chilly morning. Heavy snow is predicted for the third day in a row. I certainly do not mind. In fact, the timing of this winter storm could not be more fortuitous—I need a week of enforced hibernation in my cottage.

It has been a productive week so far, despite my occasional lapses into avoidance behavior. As a solo consultant, avoidance behavior (any kind of sabotaging activity that seduces me into doing something other than what I am supposed to be doing, albeit just as productive in the long run) is an occupational hazard. These are the times that I long for a personal secretary or administrative assistant to keep me on the straight and narrow! Not wanting to support the additional overhead, however, I constantly need to monitor myself and to enforce self-discipline.

The telephone rings. I am about to complete a follow-up report for a client. I listen to the "screener" of my answering machine and decide to pick up. It is my colleague, asking me to submit a proposal by tomorrow! It seems like a simple enough request. Instead of staying on track and completing the work that I have already started, I fall into an old trap. It happens so quickly.

I allotted an hour to prepare the proposal. Before I knew it, my quick proposal took on a life of its own. I was so caught up in it that an hour and a half had passed. I plea-bargained (with myself) for another fifteen minutes, and after several more attempts took myself to task.

I knew, all the while, that I should stop, but I was fully engaged. Ideas were flowing. Inertia was carrying me along. I forged ahead, fueled by my increasing energy level. I could hardly wait to see the finished proposal. With so many projects going at once, I struggle to regularly remind myself to pull back and contain my excitement.

Having faxed the proposal, I return to my follow-up report. The report was to be a "gift," although it was contracted for in advance. Preparing a detailed and extensive report was my way of saying "thank you." Working with this client and her organization had been an unusually positive experience. The client, in this case an "energized other" (Weisbord, 1987), made me want to go the extra mile and help her realize her dreams. We had worked together for over eight months preparing the organization and developing the format for this workshop. It had gone well. I had done exactly what we agreed I would do: empowered the group and left them with plenty to think about. The client's expectations had been met. The workshop was not just an organizational booster shot but rather problem-posing (Freire, 1970), dialogic (Mezirow, 1981), and self-directed (Brookfield, 1986) learning, which promotes and sustains organizational development and change.

My basic practice assumption is that just as individuals can be empowered through learning, so too can groups and organizations. I know I have been effective when I work myself out of a job and turn the group on to the power of its own resources. Perhaps the one thing that I find most satisfying and joyful is this generative aspect of my consulting business, when I am able to help a group turn on to itself, unleash its own creative energies, and mobilize itself to action.

I am wary about getting involved with clients who are not patient with process and collaborative learning, because these are two key generative elements. For me, the collective wisdom that results from the unique contributions of individuals is the major force for transforming individual participants into viable learning communities.

Given the varying range of clients' perceptions of consultants, it is essential that my clients understand what my role is as a facilitator. Getting others to understand not only who I am but what it is I do are basic to marketing, design, implementation, and quality consulting service.

It took me many years of becoming confident in and comfortable with my own identity as a consultant before I achieved success. At first, I operated by instinct, doing what felt right. There was no normative model for my practice. I did not know of any other adult education consultant colleagues. I was amazed to find out years later that others were feeling the same kind of professional loneliness that I felt! My professional life today is exciting and never boring. I deal with many different publics and constantly meet new people. I have had to make choices along the way. I have had to learn that I could not be "all things to all people."

I do not need to play the political games of organizational life. I do not report to a boss. I call my own shots. But, there is also the downside. I *am* my own shop! In a sense, I have multiple bosses. My contracts are subject to multiple entities' economic exigencies in addition to fluctuations of the marketplace.

I often describe my role as that of a "pointer-outer" (Lindeman, 1926) or a symphony conductor helping people to "touch and feel" (DePree,

1992) as they act. My agenda at all times is to *facilitate learning*. Weisbord's (1987, p. 277) third-wave question is always in the forefront of my mind: "What structures make it possible for people to do learning, futuring, and action planning for themselves?" For me, good consulting is synonymous with good adult education. My starting point is always "where the learner is" (Lindeman, 1926).

I am grateful for the snow day. I feel refreshed and reinvigorated. Is it possible to schedule a snow day in July?

Spring: Early One April Morning

It is 6:30 A.M. I want to start the day "on the right foot" with a brisk early morning walk. I know it is going to be a full day and if I do not take that walk now, I shall never find the time later.

Nothing like a brisk walk first thing in the morning to get me up and going. The chirping birds and the ducks in the nearby pond are sure indicators that spring is at long last here!

As I come out of the shower, I hear the faint echoes of the "fax mating call." By the time I finish breakfast, the answering machine has rung several times. With each ring, I resist the temptation to listen, deciding instead to digest my breakfast and commune with Bryant Gumbel and Katie Couric.

It is 8:30 A.M. Time to get to work. It is definitely a sweatshirt workday, a welcome change from the normal formality of my public persona. Although I have scheduled no meetings, a glance at my "day-timer" reveals that, once again, there is far too much to do and not enough time. I am not complaining. I would rather feel like an octopus than have no tentacles at all!

The telephone rings. It is a new client wanting to talk about a board development workshop. Am I interested? I am, but I want to know more. As we talk, I begin to suspect some underlying organizational problems. This may not be a client I want to take on. I ask for more information and make an appointment to talk later next week, needing to do some home-work before I agree to work with them.

As I hang up, my other telephone line rings. I wonder how long it will be before I give in and install voice mail. It is clear that I shall have to do something soon. No more time to wonder, the fax machine has just delivered an immediate-reply request from a colleague.

Before I finally settle down to my escalating "to do" list, I glance at the proposal in progress in my in-basket. I am excited because it presents the kind of opportunity I like best: to be generative, to be genuinely creative, and to learn about a whole new content area of knowledge.

The phone rings. It is Jim, returning my follow-up call. Jim and I have touched base several times in the past few years. He keeps talking about "all the business" he has for me, but for some reason it has not materialized. His folder has been in my "potential client" file for over two years now. It looks now as if Jim is going to make good on his promise. He wants me to deliver a training workshop for his staff next month. Now, I am in a quandary. How do I charge? I have already given away telephone consultation time in preparation for the workshop. I am sure that some of his needs and organizational personnel have changed since we started talking, which means added preparation time. I want to schedule him as soon as possible for I know full well that if I put him off, the opportunity may not present itself for another two years.

I spend an enormous amount of time on the front end preparing for workshops and training sessions. This is critical, particularly when I facilitate workshops for an annual client, because it is then that I run the risk of overassuming. It is important not to take last year's assumptions for granted this year, especially in today's climate of rapid change. The "players," the culture, and the circumstances change continuously. It is essential to allow for the growth and development of the organization and the individuals and groups within them.

Years ago, "Jim situations" would not have put me in a quandary. I would have just charged the client what I quoted originally and put in whatever time was necessary to do the job. Experience has been a wise teacher. I set a date for a face-to-face meeting with Jim. It is time to renegotiate.

Recently, an article I read (Caffarella, 1993) triggered reflection on my own adult development and learning as a consultant over the past years. I am beginning to see how theory applies to my own development as an adult education consultant. There are discrete stages of development that progress from externality as a novice to internality or locus of control as one matures in the role. In the early years, when I was establishing myself, I would accept everything that anybody asked me to do. I would give away my time, hoping to recoup it in future business. Today I am more circumspect. I have learned to value my time and services. I still give time away but I am more selective. I choose the pro bono work I do because that is the way I can give value-added service as a volunteer.

As I write, I realize that I need to reflect more about these developmental passages. I had better build some time and space into my calendar. Maybe over the summer. . .

Summer: A Hot Day in July

It is a quiet day, but then that is how I have planned it. I have scheduled time to catch up: to read professional journals, to finish a popular new book on leadership, and to write an article. I have been on the road twice already this month. Next week I am scheduled for two back-to-back trips. Generally, I try to avoid this kind of frenetic pace by leaving a day in between clients. Doing that also gives me a chance to get up to speed and shift gears.

Catch-up days always energize and challenge me. Unfortunately, they are few and far between, despite my best intentions. By setting aside big blocks of uninterrupted time, I am able to keep myself current, continually reflect on my practice (Schön, 1983) through writing, and bring some real creativity to my consulting practice.

Writing is an important part of my professional life. Writing helps me to crystallize my thinking and apply new learning to my practice. It enables me to continuously improve as a professional. I do not need to publish for tenure or promotion. Writing meets my professional need to share my learning and experiences with colleagues. It is my way of giving back to colleagues in the profession some of what they have given me.

I hear a voice on the answering machine in the distance. I am trying to ignore it, but hearing the familiar voice of a colleague reminds me of the last board meeting we attended. It was actually a half-day retreat, which, to put it kindly, was poorly executed. I remember sitting in my seat consciously resisting the urge to get up and fix it by facilitating the process. I find it hard to let go of my professional role and completely enter someone else's process. It is particularly problematic when things go awry. When things go well, I find myself participating more as an observer and student of process technique. One of the liabilities of being a consultant, for me, is compromising my full participation and subconsciously shutting down because I am so conditioned to *being* the process person.

Today, I am writing about my experience facilitating women's leadership groups, specifically my observations about how some women's groups mirror the stages of women's development. A group with which I recently worked played out the metaphors of "voice," "connection," and "caring" (Gilligan, 1982; Belenky, Clinchy, Goldberger, and Tarule, 1986). They found themselves stuck in transition. By taking developmental theory and teaching group members how to hold it up as a lens, they were able to better understand how the organization was functioning. They learned why and how they got stuck and how to move the group from one stage of development to the next. It was a fascinating process for all of us. As I review the notes, I realize how much the construct of "voice" informs my practice, in the group setting as well as in others. My role as a consultant is to bring out others' voices by raising the questions and issues that someone from the inside of the organization cannot or will not.

I turn my head and my eyes focus on the sign on my office door, which says "My other office has a window." I walk upstairs and see sunshine streaming through the windows. I was almost convinced it was January! One of the perks of being a consultant is the sense of freedom I experience in being able to create my own snow days. Enough musing. It is time for a break!

Fall: An Indian Summer Afternoon

The days are getting shorter and busier. I have just returned from a private reception. During the reception, I talked with Craig, whom I have known for many years. I was surprised when he suddenly asked me, "Just what is it you do anyway? I don't understand. I know you travel a lot and you give presentations, but what do you do?" After I explained to him that I facilitate adult learning and gave him concrete examples from other settings, he responded, "Well, if you can do that for them, can you do that for me in my small business?" I had never thought about a small publishing business as part of my market. But the more he talked, the more I realized that through that conversation another window of opportunity had been opened. He invited me to meet with his partners the following week. I learned again that, as consultants, we cannot assume people know what we do. We need to always tell the story in different ways. Getting people to understand who I am is sometimes difficult, since my clients know me in different contexts. The lessons to be learned are these: (1) Getting out and around is "good exposure," (2) each contact is a potential customer, (3) an old friend may turn out to be the next customer, and (4) if people are to *understand* what we do for a living, they must be told in terms to which they can relate.

The telephone rings again and I cradle it to my ear with my shoulder. As I finish writing my note, I listen to the caller. It is the callback I have been waiting for on a proposal that I submitted last April. Yes, they want to hire me as a consultant/trainer for the next six months, but "the money is a problem." They ask if I would consider doing the consulting and training for less than I quoted. I ask what that means. It is suggested that I lower my fee by doing less consulting and more training. "The fact is we only have 'x' dollars to spend." I am concerned about maintaining the integrity of the process: How do I do half as much and still get a quality outcome? I make a case for building ownership as necessary groundwork for supporting the outcomes of the workshop. They are not buying this argument. I suggest that perhaps they need to be less ambitious or lower their expectations if they truly want me to do half as much.

How and when to make compromises always raises financial, professional, and personal issues for which there are no hard and fast rules. I need to think more about this conversation. Perhaps I should turn down the work and suggest another consultant I know who is not as concerned about process? This is clearly a prospective client who has little understanding of my role and who will not be satisfied with my product.

A mutual understanding of the consultant's role is reinforced by how payment for services is handled. Usually, the client has a paycheck ready for me after delivery of a training workshop or within ten days. Payment signals closure, and it is how we both know that further work needs to be renegotiated. Clients who delay payment are often the same clients who practice what I call the "extraction theory of consultant utilization," always calling me for advice—asking me to do something else or often saying, "As long as you are here why don't you . . . ?"

Today, I look at that situation from a different perspective. Clients' lack of understanding about my role may reflect their reluctance to let go or simply their lack of self-confidence. A written agreement has been a successful way to handle this situation. The agreement details my role and responsibilities as well as theirs, how much specific services will cost, and a "pay by . . . " date.

No sooner do I hang up, but another call rings through. It is not the call I was expecting. Sure enough, the other line rings. (Why did I pick it up?) Suddenly, I find myself back-to-back on two calls at once. I should know better than to do the telephone trapeze act. I cannot give my full attention to either. I reschedule the first call and focus on the second, a colleague from a nearby community. She has called to tell me that our networking group will meet the following week. What did I want to put on the agenda? What did I need feedback and support on? Given the hectic pace of the day, I was delighted that she had assumed responsibility for the meeting logistics.

As promised, I return the other telephone call. (I must confess, sometimes I do feel as though the telephone is a permanent appendage to my ear!) It is one of my long-term clients, who asks if I would attend an organizational meeting of a task force that he is trying to put in place, "as long as I'm coming into the office anyway." He does not ask for "extras" very often; and when he does, I always know it will be worth my time. I agree to attend and rearrange my schedule accordingly. (I am not always so quick to respond to a client's request.)

Just as I put my pen down, the telephone rings again. It is someone calling to request a workshop. As I listen to her request, I become uneasy. My gut is telling me not to get involved. She is not answering any of the questions I ask her. I sense that she will be difficult to communicate with and that the "chemistry" just is not there. I listen politely and recommend someone else for the job.

I resist the temptation to move on to the next file. I look at the technomaze that surrounds me, disbelieving how much I have come to depend on all of this high-tech equipment. I write a memo to myself, outlining what is left undone. I glance at tomorrow's schedule and pack up my briefcase so that I am ready to leave my cottage early in the morning. It is 6:30 P.M. I turn out the light. Tomorrow is another day.

This Is a Living!

The competing demands of my consulting practice force me to continually reassess my business operations as well as my practice. For example, when

I reread my diary entries, I am struck by the extent of my involvement with and dependence on the telephone. It is, to a very real extent, my lifeline. Time and reasonable scheduling are also issues for me. Learning how to make these and other occupational and operational issues work for me is a constant challenge.

I realize how important it is for me to get others to understand who I am, what it is I do, and what my role is to be as "their" consultant. Despite occasional struggles with the operational and process aspects of my business, I find consulting an enormously satisfying profession. This is a living! And I reaffirm my commitment by choosing to continue doing it. I like the challenges it presents, the people I meet, and the opportunities for personal and professional growth it provides. It enables me to bring a range of skills into focus that stir others to action on their own behalf. I add the richness of the adult learning perspective, which is value added to those who hire me, since it is desired and timely in today's climate of learning organizations.

The work of a consultant requires a constant balancing act, an openness in the face of changing demands, and continuous learning. It also requires self-motivation, self-discipline, patience, and a belief in the promise that adult learning holds: Through adult learning, individuals, groups, and organizations have the potential to grow, develop, and reach beyond the present to create a more meaningful future for themselves and for others.

References

Belenky, M. F., Clinchy, B. M., Goldberger, N. R., and Tarule, J. M. *Women's Ways of Knowing: The Development of Self, Voice, and Mind.* New York: Basic Books, 1986.

Brookfield, S. D. *Understanding and Facilitating Adult Learning: A Comprehensive Analysis of Principles and Effective Practices.* San Francisco: Jossey-Bass, 1986.

Cafferella, R. S. "The Continuing Journey of Our Professional Lives." *Adult Learning,* 1993, 4 (3), 27, 30.

DePree, M. *Leadership Jazz.* New York: Doubleday, 1992.

Freire, P. *Pedagogy of the Oppressed.* New York: Continuum, 1970.

Gilligan, C. *In a Different Voice: Psychological Theory and Women's Development.* Cambridge, Mass.: Harvard University Press, 1982.

Lindeman, E. C. *The Meaning of Adult Education.* New York: Harvest Books, 1926.

Mezirow, J. "A Critical Theory of Adult Learning and Education." *Adult Education,* 1981, 32 (1), 3–27.

Naisbitt, J. *Megatrends.* New York: Warner, 1982.

Schön, D. A. *The Reflective Practitioner: How Professionals Think in Action.* New York: Basic Books, 1983.

Weisbord, M. R. *Productive Workplaces: Organizing and Managing for Dignity, Meaning, and Community.* San Francisco: Jossey-Bass, 1987.

LOIS J. ZACHARY is an education consultant with a private consulting practice in Fayetteville, New York.

The importance of developing and nurturing professional relationships for an effective adult education consulting practice is highlighted.

Developing and Nurturing Professional Relationships

William A. Howe

Like many others who have made the same decision, for me the process of becoming a full-time, independent consultant was both a thrilling and a terrifying experience. On the one hand, there was the relief of not having a boss and not having to deal with the bureaucracy of an organization. On the other hand, the darker side, I was coming to the stark realization as I sat at my desk in my new home office that I had no one to talk to! There was no one to answer my phone, open my mail, or do the photocopying and filing. Becoming an independent consultant in adult education may be seen as an ultimate test of the theories behind self-directed learning as proposed by Tough (1979) and Brookfield (1986). It certainly requires undertaking many new learning projects and turning to others for help.

Unless one is fortunate enough to begin a business with an established clientele, boredom and anxiety can set in. To be a successful independent consultant, one must offer a service or product of high caliber and have access to information about current best practices. One of the greatest fears of being in business on one's own is loss of contact with what is happening beyond the walls of one's office. The lack of a support system results in feelings of isolation and loneliness and less vitality and enthusiasm for the important work that must be done. It is ironic that "collaborative learning," a basic tenet of adult education (Marsick, 1987), is often elusive to the independent practitioner.

It need not be elusive, however. The following are suggestions on how to develop and nurture collaborative learning, as an independent practitioner, through professional relationships with other private consultants. The suggestions include reading the right journals, seeking the right clubs or

New Directions for Adult and Continuing Education, no. 58, Summer 1993 © Jossey-Bass Publishers

organizations to join, and maintaining a network of contacts in organizations and businesses. They address two general need areas common to private consultants: development of technical expertise and establishment of collegial and collaborative relationships, which encompasses aspects of professional identity and emotional support.

Development of Technical Expertise

A necessary skill for adult education consultants is familiarity with and effective use of resources that support their practices. Some of the resources discussed here include reference books and journals and human resources.

Finding Book Resources. Although public and academic libraries should be used as much as possible, consultants in private practice each need a personal library of professional reference materials. There are some classics and general reference books that should be available on an ongoing basis. These can be categorized as general technical (reference books for use by writers in general), content references (reference books that relate to one's specialized business, such as nursing or financial advice), and practice references (reference books that support the actual process of consulting).

General technical resources include standard works such as a dictionary, a thesaurus, a world and nationwide atlas, and almanacs. To add spice to one's writing and lectures, a good book of quotations, such as *Bartlett's Familiar Quotations* (Bartlett and Kaplan, 1992), is often very helpful. Another good source to have on hand is one that documents specific events in history, such as *What Happened When: A Chronology of Life and Events in America* (Carruth, 1991).

There are excellent all-around references that bridge adult education and training. *The Trainer's Professional Development Handbook* (Bard, Bell, Stephen, and Webster, 1987) covers much of the "how-to" of setting up a practice. It also contains chapters on topics such as the best books in the field of training; journals, newsletters, periodicals, and indexes; professional organizations and associations; and conferences, workshops, and academic programs.

The *Handbook of Adult and Continuing Education* (Merriam and Cunningham, 1989) provides an excellent review of adult education. It offers a broad perspective of the field, which can serve as a guide to developing and expanding the consultant's practice. Another general reference book that documents current training trends is the *Training and Development Yearbook, 1992/1993* (Frantzreb, 1992). This book provides a listing of recent articles and abstracts on timely topics in the field of human resources development.

For assistance in developing a business, consider *The Consultant's Calling: Bringing Who You Are to What You Do* (Bellman, 1990), *The Consummate Trainer: A Practitioner's Perspective* (Spaid, 1986), *How to Succeed as an*

Independent Consultant (Holtz, 1990), *Marketing Your Consulting and Professional Services* (Connor and Davidson, 1985), and *Secrets of a Successful Trainer: A Simplified Guide to Survival* (Lambert, 1986). All of these "easy reading" books provide a wealth of practical information, including marketing strategies, personal development, business tips, presentation skills, and resources for the independent consultant.

Choosing Subscriptions to Periodicals. When beginning a full-time consulting business, money is often limited. Subscriptions to journals and magazines must be purchased sparingly if these are not available through another source.

Periodicals can be divided into three categories: those for academic needs, those for content expertise, and those for dealing with the management of a business. Academic journals and series, such as *Adult Education Quarterly* and New Directions for Adult and Continuing Education, offer theoretical perspectives pertinent to consultants in higher education. Content expertise periodicals include *Training Magazine* (Lakewood Publications) and *Training and Development Journal* (American Society for Training and Development). These two journals are the training industry standards. They contain timely articles on innovations in the training profession, including presentation skills, management theories, and technologies. The journal *Adult Learning* (American Association on Adult and Continuing Education) also addresses practical ideas and approaches, with a strong focus on adult basic education and literacy. Journals that offer aid in developing and maintaining a small business, such as *Home Office Computing,* cover diverse topics such as marketing techniques, office design, and technology.

The "glamor magazines" can also be of help to the adult education consultant. Articles on stress management, personal communication, and other useful topics frequently appear in this literature.

Using the Library. Public libraries are often unrecognized as valuable resources. The benefits of using the library are many. For example, a good reference librarian who takes an interest in a consultant's subject matter is an extremely valuable resource. The library also offers computer access to books and periodicals, book borrowing nationwide, reading rooms, and reference books. Some states (such as Colorado and Illinois) allow access to library catalogues via modem, which is an excellent way to conduct cost- and time-efficient literature searches. Interlibrary loans are another way of expanding access to resources. A major benefit is that all of these services are free.

Establishment of Collegial and Collaborative Relationships

A network of professional colleagues and a personal support system are vital to a successful consulting practice.

Adjunct Faculty Appointments. Most universities and community colleges have not only continuing education departments but also departments that specifically provide training and consultation services to business and industry. Adjunct faculty or contractual lecturers are routinely hired to provide these services. The benefits of maintaining an association with institutions of higher education are numerous. They offer opportunities for consultants to gain visibility, to engage in dialogue with colleagues, and to work collaboratively toward mutually beneficial ends.

Local Adult Education Programs. Local adult education programs usually offer a wide variety of continuing education courses. Because of the broad range of courses offered and the diversity of the clientele served, these programs offer good opportunities for consultants to market their expertise and establish collegial networks.

Associates. Many consultants have chosen to form associations with other independent consultants. Each can act as a subcontractor and referral source for the others, and the base of expertise is thereby broadened for all. In addition, an opportunity is provided to develop and nurture connections with associates who are a source of technical information, emotional support, and referrals and potential partners in joint work projects and the writing of books and articles.

Publishing. Name recognition is one of the keys to success. To establish credibility, consultants can start with simple "letters to the editor" in their market areas. Trade journals are often seeking authors with expertise congruent with the interests of their readership. Consultants have access through libraries to vast collections of journals. Do not hesitate to nurture relationships with representatives of appropriate journals that might provide publishing possibilities. Discuss potential topics for publication with the representatives and be sure to ask for and adhere to the publication guidelines of individual journals. Remember, the main idea is to develop a professional identity and presence as an adult education consultant.

Personal Support System. Friends and family are an integral part of a consultant's support network. Because they tend to affirm personal strengths, they enhance the potential for professional growth. They often provide the kind of objective feedback and sustenance necessary to achieve a balanced perspective.

Conclusion

Individuals who are considering adult education consulting as a career are well advised to revisit the literature on self-directed learning. In this way, they can better prepare themselves for the realities of practice and better position themselves to reap the full rewards and benefits of a growing area of adult education practice.

In order to thrive, consultants must develop and nurture many types of relationships. These include peers, colleagues, friends, and family. The benefit of connections with these individuals and the maximum utilization of resources and networks is personal and professional satisfaction.

References

Bard, R., Bell, C. R., Stephen, L., Webster, L. *The Trainer's Professional Development Handbook*. San Francisco: Jossey-Bass, 1987.

Bartlett, J., and Kaplan, J. *Bartlett's Familiar Quotations*. (16th ed.) Boston: Little, Brown, 1992.

Bellman, G. M. *The Consultant's Calling: Bringing Who You Are to What You Do*. San Francisco: Jossey-Bass, 1990.

Brookfield, S. D. *Understanding and Facilitating Adult Learning: A Comprehensive Analysis of Principles and Effective Practices*. San Francisco: Jossey-Bass, 1986.

Carruth, G. *What Happened When: A Chronology of Life and Events in America*. New York: HarperCollins, 1991.

Connor, R. A., and Davidson, J. P. *Marketing Your Consulting and Professional Services*. New York: Wiley, 1985.

Frantzreb, R. B. *Training and Development Yearbook, 1992/1993*. Englewood Cliffs, N.J.: Prentice Hall, 1992.

Holtz, H. *How to Succeed as an Independent Consultant*. New York: Wiley, 1990.

Lambert, C. L. *Secrets of a Successful Trainer: A Simplified Guide to Survival*. New York: Wiley, 1986.

Marsick, V. J. (ed.). *Learning in the Workplace*. London: Croom-Helm, 1987.

Merriam, S. B., and Cunningham, P. M. (eds.). *Handbook of Adult and Continuing Education*. San Francisco: Jossey-Bass, 1989.

Spaid, O. A. *The Consummate Trainer: A Practitioner's Perspective*. Englewood Cliffs, N.J.: Prentice Hall, 1986.

Tough, A. M. *The Adult's Learning Projects: A Fresh Approach to Theory and Practice in Adult Learning*. (2nd ed.) Toronto: Ontario Institute for Studies in Education, 1979.

WILLIAM A. HOWE *is director of the Connecticut Department of Children and Youth Services Training Academy and has his own consulting firm in Glastonbury.*

Technology is essential in establishing and maintaining a consulting practice.

Developing and Maintaining Contact with Clients

William T. Vericker

Relationship building is critical to a consulting practice. Most consultants would agree that it makes good business sense to establish contacts through multiple venues. Contacts are critical to developing a constant stream of clients. What most consultants have not fully realized, however, is the benefit to be derived through judicious use of technology and automation. Technology offers a cost-effective and personalized way of building and maintaining relationships. This chapter describes how I bring in business, maintain the relationships that I establish, and use technology to support the relationship aspects of my business.

Bringing in Business

As president of my own company, I am supported by clerical and professional staff. In the last several years, we have come into contact with thousands of potential clients—individuals whom we have met through a variety of conventions, trade shows, and referrals. My goal is to have *all* of my potential clients know who I am, my message, and what benefits they can expect from my company's services. My staff and I work toward this goal by integrating the best that technology has to offer with personal contact.

Every encounter is a contact point. There are several rules that we follow concerning our speaking engagements. We work at obtaining the correct salutations or "nicknames" of the people we meet. It is remarkable to me the number of my own colleagues whose mailing lists carry only the formal names or salutations of individuals and not the names that these individuals actually use in their daily lives. This is also true with titles such as "Doctor" and professional designations that may be significant, particularly in relation to the businesses and industries in which the clients work.

It is our practice to establish a variety of mailing lists, and to categorize them for repeat mailings, so that we can send personalized contact letters to every name on the lists. For example, for seminars, we establish a mailing list of all of the attendees of the program, make certain that each salutation is correct, and within seventy-two hours remind attendees that the information learned at the seminar can be translated into cost savings, productivity increases, additional learning opportunities, or other value-added services if implemented and enhanced after the seminar experience. Since, in our experience, the sales cycle on consulting is either extremely short or extremely long, the seventy-two-hour follow-up letter is targeted to highly motivated clients, those who either immediately wish to obtain our services or call directly after receiving a letter, brochure, or business card from our firm. Typically, they call and ask us to set up the same exact service that was described in the seminar. It is not unusual for us to receive several responses, which lead to five to seven billable days of work, from seminars where attendance was no greater than twenty-five people.

As mentioned, the sales cycle for consulting is, in our experience, either extremely short or extremely long. Those clients on the longer cycle often gather information about several consultants, decide at some point whom and what they need, and contact their consultant of choice. To increase the possibility that this client will call us, we use technology to maintain a steady stream of contact. We send regularly timed, written contacts, once again with the correct salutations, reminding them of earlier correspondence, the content of previous seminars, and, in particular, the benefits that can be derived from our services.

We do a general mailing at the end of each calendar year to all of our clients, particularly those with whom we have not had regular contact. In this letter, we typically forecast bleak or dismal economic times, the need for independent and self-directed learning and organizational change, and the savings to the organization that can be obtained by setting up employee manuals, individualized training plans and contracts, efficiency and effectiveness studies, and general reorganization. Since the bulk of my practice seems to be organized around organizational development and self-directed learning activities, I have found that the mere thought of their December 31 numbers, and reduced incomes, is often sufficient motivation for them to hire a consultant to come in and fix their problems.

My consultant calendar fills in one of two ways. Like most smaller firms, we find that it is critical to maintain a relatively high profile and visibility in the industries in which we work. On a yearly basis, I speak at approximately fifteen annual conventions of various state, regional, and national associations; my topics are often employees and how to improve their performance, individual and organizational learning, staff management, and reorganization. I always try to speak to the local trade, press, or newspaper reporters on assignment at the conventions. I provide outlines of my speeches before I give them, and, if necessary, I provide related articles or summaries, to make the job of reviewing the contents of my speech, workshop, or general-session seminar presentation easier for the participant.

In terms of later contact with attendees at these events, for the largest of conventions my staff and I simply bring brochures and business cards and suggest, at the end of the presentation, that anyone wishing to ask further questions contact us. I find that most conference sponsors are unwilling to give consultants full attendee lists or the mailing lists that they use to send conference announcements and invitations to individuals. I generally prefer not to use others' mailing lists, since I find them impersonal and prefer to have the letters individually and appropriately addressed.

My presentations at the fifteen annual conventions generally lead to the retainment of my services for topic-oriented seminars, which I conduct approximately three or four times each month. In these seminars, I meet individuals with whom I work one-on-one, often in groups of less than fifty, and on topics that are always geared toward benefit-driven consulting. If participants implement the concepts taught in these seminars, I can guarantee that they will save money. These individuals also receive follow-up letters, brochures, business cards, and a preprinted list of references from our most successful clients.

Continuing the Contact

Each and every one of our lists are coded so that we can go back and send another letter, usually at thirty-, sixty-, or ninety-day intervals. In our experience, there is a certain slippage in the enthusiasm of individuals, and the thirty-day contact sometimes motivates them to call us. Our sixty- and ninety-day follow-ups generate the same level of response as the thirty-day follow-ups.

Where the sales cycle is particularly long, I contribute articles to trade journals, national publications, and business-related magazines. This is one more attempt to associate my name with the consulting that potential clients will some day require.

The clients that always strike fear, and consequent joy, in the hearts of most consultants are the people who wait three months, six months, nine months, or even two years to call. However, when they do call, they are finally ready and always want the consultant to visit them tomorrow. Since no consultant ever wants to work with anything other than a motivated client, I make every effort to schedule a visit with them as soon as possible to begin the consulting relationship. Once again, we have a series of standard contact and marketing letters in which we outline the requirements of consulting, and what we expect from the client prior to our visit.

There are times when we could use our mailing-list technology better. We work smart, using the simplest of word-processing programs, and make certain that our lists include both the nature of each group, generally identified by the character letter of the name and mailing list, as well as some sort of demographic information, even if only zip code. We have developed a series of "blind-mailer" letters, in which we announce the availability of a particular client or individual program and encourage the recipients of the letters to contact us for further information. These letters are often sent by using a zip code, state code, or local regional sort on the various mailing lists that we maintain.

Maintaining Contact with Clients

There are several factors that must be considered when maintaining contact with clients. First, in addition to the appropriate timing of correspondence, the content must *always* be totally benefit-oriented and drive home the message that any money spent on consulting will accomplish the dual objectives of translating seminar action into real activity and of recouping fees paid to the consulting firm through the savings in personnel, training, and other expenses.

Second, convention speeches, magazine articles, and marketing letters eventually wind up in a file with the consulting firm's name on it, and it is that file that a potential client often turns to when he or she finally has a question.

Third, I answer questions from clients, particularly new clients, on a first-time, first-phone-call basis, without billing for anywhere under fifteen minutes of my time. Should individuals meet me at a seminar and later call for clarifications or to ask questions, I state right up front that I would love to speak with them and I would love to answer their questions, but, as I tell them in the most pleasant and humorous of ways, "the free advice clock is ticking, and it has a short tick span." I generally try to provide just enough information to interest the client in my services. These, like all other contacts, are immediately followed up by a letter, coded for recontact within thirty days.

Consulting: A Personal Relationship Business

There is no question that a consulting practice in adult learning, organizational development, or a related area is a personal relationship business. Individuals need to feel comfortable with consultants, their reputations, their professionalism, and their expertise. Technology keeps the contact going and thus helps consultants maintain relationships. I am convinced that steady personalized contact, generated through technology and combined face-to-face interaction, helps consultants achieve this goal. Therefore, I maintain a booth at three diverse trade shows during the course of each year. I have my booth material ready, collect business cards in exchange for a free gift, and initiate written contact as soon as possible. I do not take a business card from any individual without the proper salutation to load in the word-processing system. Once again, those contacts receive an immediate marketing letter. If I really feel that there is a "hot opportunity" for the future, I am certain to telephone or follow up in some other fashion.

Professionalism, expertise, and ability to help clients are very important, but they are lost if consultants are unable to develop and maintain relationships with their clients. They will never be given an opportunity to demonstrate their competence if they cannot get "through the door." Stationery, logo, brochures, business cards, and references help create the image that opens that door.

When I first started my consulting business, I was told that, as a rule of thumb, 20 percent of my time should be devoted to marketing. The longer I have been in business, the more convinced I have become that building, maintaining, and contacting client lists demands *at least* 20 percent of one's time. Technology allows consultants a great number of sorts and profiles of the lists that they maintain. It allows the option of targeting by zip code, area, business type, or any combination thereof.

Use of support staff keeps the cost of regular multiple contacts inexpensive and extremely productive. I realize that if I invest three or four hours of secretarial time, thereby generate fifty to seventy-five personalized contacts, and from that effort generate several clients, I have not only paid for the time expended but also benefited from relatively low marketing costs.

Consulting relationships are personal. Since contact is critical, my staff and I ensure that telephone contacts are just as personalized and helpful as our letter contacts. We have a series of voice-mail systems that answer the telephone when no one is available or when both incoming lines are busy. We have two lines dedicated to clients. If both are busy, we utilize an answer-call system through which our clients receive the following message: "You've reached Vericker and Associates, and unfortunately, all of our incoming lines are busy at this moment. We are in the office, and your call is important to us. If you leave your name and a phone number, we will get back to you quickly. Please wait for the beep." As soon as we hang up, we are beeped, pick up the message, and return the call faithfully. Clients come to know this, and the message "all of our incoming lines are busy" connotes a large bustling firm.

I debated with myself about the need for voice mail or any form of message machine. However, when I attended a small business seminar, I received the best piece of information that I have ever received. "People hate voice mail," I was told, "because they never know if you are in Bermuda or in the bathroom." I change the incoming message at least once a day. It always gives important information to the caller, particularly when the client can expect a call back. No one expects to get an answer on the first ring, but clients do like to know when they will hear from us. A typical message might say, "I am traveling today, Monday, January 4th, and will not check my messages until late this afternoon. If you leave a message, I will call you back either later today or first thing tomorrow morning." I try to check for messages and return calls when I say I am going to. I get compliments all the time on this system, which is no more sophisticated than a good answering machine and voice mail from the local telephone company. I also use my car phone to check messages or to return urgent calls. So I am rarely out of contact. Our clients appreciate the voice-mail option. It helps to build and strengthen their relationships with us.

Constancy

The use of technology to develop and nurture professional relationships is a necessity in establishing and maintaining a consulting practice. Word-processing, mail-merge, and mailing-list generation capabilities are invaluable. But technology alone does not suffice. Continuous follow-up is required. Constancy is also a necessity. The trick is to "keep at it," market strategically, and utilize benefit-driven contacts. For us, technology has facilitated personal contact, which has enhanced our business immeasurably.

WILLIAM T. VERICKER is president of his own consulting firm in Hillsdale, New York.

It is possible to hold a full-time academic position and at the same time develop a thriving consulting practice.

Getting the Best of Both Worlds

Norma S. Friedman

> There is a history of leaders and groups who are ahead of their time, who resist prevailing trends, but who appear in the official accounts as misinformed or malintentioned obstacles to the main direction of historical development. There is a history of 'commonfolk' struggling to become, and becoming, their own leaders.
>
> —Frank Adams (1972, p. 497)

As a tenured professor in a small business and engineering college in the Midwest, I have the luxury of thinking about and practicing the art of adult education. The teaching of my four courses a semester can be an oasis of theory and technique continuously refined and focused to my satisfaction. I regularly read and study the history, data, trends, demographics, and theoretical orientations of academics and scholars.

It is, however, my other job, a thriving consulting practice, that gives me the opportunity to meet the people who are struggling, succeeding, and changing the social fabric of our culture. They are not yet in the literature of any field or in history books, and may never be, but they are the movers and shakers of education, arts, and social services who daily change their worlds and enrich mine. More than supplementing my teaching, this second career complements and energizes my daily teaching activities.

Multiple work responsibilities in and out of one's home institution do present special challenges. In this chapter, I examine some of the issues that I have confronted as an adult educator holding a full-time academic position and providing consultation and training independently of an institutional affiliation.

The attraction of the field of adult education to many of us is its orientation toward change and development of both individuals and com-

NEW DIRECTIONS FOR ADULT AND CONTINUING EDUCATION, no. 58, Summer 1993 © Jossey-Bass Publishers

munity. The context and practice of adult education are both linked directly to the community. Brookfield (1984) has created a typology linking adult education and community that identifies three practice approaches: adult education for the community, adult education in the community, and adult education of the community. In the first approach, adult educators program activities based on desires of individuals who are influenced by institutional bias and financial limitations. In the second approach, adult educators act more as resources and advisers to learners. In the third approach, the adult educator assesses individual and community needs and fosters individual and community self-help.

Philosophy

It is my belief that adult education attracts many practitioners because it is an arena where we can explore and practice our own idealistic and social change activism, a space where we are adult educators of the community. It is here that I see an intersection between adult education philosophy, on the one hand, and community organizing and development, on the other. Both adult educators and community organizers attempt to help individuals "regain some measure of power over a world seemingly out of control" (Boyte, 1980, p. 3). My consulting practice provides me with opportunities to use my adult education skills and change agent orientation to help individuals and organizations change and develop.

Practice

My consulting practice consists primarily of not-for-profit, government organizations and for-profit human services corporations. In addition, I am a trustee educator and consultant with Trustee Leadership Development Program, a national leadership education program funded by the Lilly Endowment. The organizations and individuals working in these arenas are constantly struggling with limited funding, changing tax bases, and fiscal constraints while grappling with profound questions of how to serve, how to empower, and how to change and improve the human condition in the face of increasing needs. In some cases it is the struggle and the smallest of successes that ignites their passion and mine for this kind of work.

The fact that I have a full-time job, a stable source of income, and few self-imposed financial pressures affects the nature and style of my consulting work. I can function as a consultant and not be solely dependent on financial remuneration from every billable hour. Thus, I can provide advice without consideration of personal financial gain. As a result, initial consultations with clients are less pressured and more authentic because I have the luxury of providing guidance, help, and advice without the burden of financial concerns. It may well be that the best advice I can give about a certain problem is simple, a solution that can be implemented without external consultation and training. In some cases, I can make a referral to an agency or service that provides programs without cost. In others, the organization needs to develop and grow, and the best strategy is to find a trustee or board member in the community who has the particular expertise needed and can donate his or her time. Occasionally, I am able to provide consultation that does not require an organization to enter into a fee-based relationship with me. This type of consulting practice resonates with my personal philosophy of adult education of the community (Brookfield, 1984). I am committed to providing assistance and advice that can empower an individual or organization to be self-sufficient while navigating oppressive social constraints.

Servant Leadership

Much of the work that I do as a private consultant and as a trustee educator and consultant is grounded in Robert Greenleaf's (1970) philosophy of servant leadership, Parker Palmer's thoughtful critiques of interventions with adult learners, and Katherine Tyler Scott's synthesis of the nature of leading, serving, and consulting (see Lemler and others, 1990). The theoretical underpinnings of servant leadership speak directly to adult educators and to consultants who pursue their work for more than financial gain. Serving is the idea of helping, caring, and doing for others, listening to and respecting the values of individuals, groups, and organizations. Leadership implies the ability to change, move, wisely use power, and show others a way. Implicit in leadership is the notion that there are followers, by virtue of either the position or the status of a leader. "Servant leadership, then, combines the power and the possibility of serving and leading together. It unites the passion for service (and passion is a very good word in Greenleaf's writing) with the action of leading. . . . Servant leadership may be exercised by individuals or by groups" (Lemler and others, 1990, p. 22).

Both consultants and adult educators are put in situations of authority. We are acknowledged as experts by role, position, or credential. At the same time, many of us have internalized our roles as servants of the common good, sometimes to the point of stagnation. We want so desperately to hear and respect our students and clients that we neglect our duty to lead. Often we equate leadership with authoritarian and tyrannical methods of management and teaching. Servant leadership has become a useful conceptual framework for both my teaching and consulting. It reconciles two seemingly contradictory roles and incorporates them into a usable and rational value system.

Logistical Issues

There are a number of logistical factors that have helped me to work full-time at an institution of higher learning and devote time to a consulting business. An important prerequisite is a "home" institution that supports its faculty in their outside interests. I have been fortunate: My institution has always supported its institutional staff in their efforts to create their own professional development activities, as long as these activities do not interfere with work responsibilities or institutional programs. Class times at my institution are blocked out according to faculty requests, which almost always are honored. This may not be true for everyone. Individual practitioners trying to manage the best of both worlds must achieve this balance according to their own institutional cultures.

Institutional flexibility is a key determinant of how successfully one can work full-time and negotiate independent consulting contracts. One additional practical consideration is the ability and desire of institutional secretarial staff to handle telephone messages. Even though I utilize a telephone answering system and private secretarial services at home, I also must work with secretarial and clerical staff at my institution.

It is equally important for me to let organizational clients know that I have institutional responsibilities, and that as much as I want to work within their schedules, I cannot always do so. It is not a matter of putting my institution over the client but rather of helping the client understand time constraints. If the service that a consultant provides is good, clients will respect institutional obligations. I always clearly state my institutional affiliation on training documents. I have been able to bring in institutional colleagues as resources and cofacilitators in various projects. Academic colleagues have been very supportive by providing resources, references, and training materials. My institutional relationship enhances my professional credentials and also promotes the mission of my institution among community leaders in both the corporate and human services arenas.

Consulting Networks

One of the greatest sources of support and intellectual stimulation is the consulting network. There are a variety of ways to begin developing such a group. The most important thing to remember is that the goals of the group need to be clearly determined and articulated.

One of my strongest support mechanisms is the Trustee Leadership Development Program. Recognizing the unique and valuable assets of independent consultants, this program provides ongoing individual resources and group training for its consultants. Not only does this particular program provide nationally recognized trainers and speakers, but it also provides opportunities for developing consultant networks.

It has become my personal imperative to have a local network of resource consultants in my area. I participate in two types of groups. First, I have an intimate group of consultant friends and contacts with whom I meet. This informal group, composed of individuals who provide consulting services on a full-time basis, provides personal support and practical advice about mutual work experiences. This group has a close connection with the local chapter of the American Society for Training and Development, which also provides me with an opportunity to discuss issues and network jobs. Second, I am a member of a group of consultants who meet monthly to discuss issues relevant to the field of consulting and to professional growth. This network is an ongoing forum for discussion of topical issues. For instance, we review books, report on conferences attended, and share resources. In reality, this second type of group may be more difficult to maintain because the goals are not as clear and it may eventually feel like one more burdensome responsibility to go to another meeting. This second group tries to ensure that everyone's personal agenda has surfaced and is attended to, or at least acknowledged, even if the group cannot develop activities to meet all individuals' needs. These types of groups can be important sources of support for independent consultants, who all too often work in isolation.

Enriching Class Content

Consulting provides an opportunity for the adult educator to connect with the realities and struggles of a community, and it provides a rich source of discussion topics and material for class. If adult education is to have meaning, it must not be empty or dry documents and words but rather living history and provocative examples of reality tied to theory. The potential of adult education as a vehicle for change rests with skillful instructors who can raise current issues for adults. Using critical analytical skills, students can attempt to develop possible solutions in a world fraught with self-interest, limited resources, and political bureaucracies. By using case histories and studies of individuals and organizations, students can reflect on and evaluate the action taken and, subsequently, understand the dilemmas that prompted those actions. In some instances, I can use my consulting work and report on the consequences of actions taken by organizations. Thus, using actual scenarios, course content is enriched. Students have the opportunity to review real-world problems as supplements to traditional class material.

The quality of my consulting also improves because each semester I have the opportunity to receive valuable feedback on my practice. Student critiques of the case studies of my organizational experiences enable me to continuously learn from their insights and opinions. My students receive additional benefits from this practice. They appreciate knowing that their views are valued, and they have the opportunity to evaluate current organizational problems.

Conclusion

Working full-time in a higher education institution and maintaining a consulting practice, I, as an adult educator, have the opportunity to integrate theory with organizational reality. The stories, documents, and passions of " 'commonfolk' struggling to become, and becoming, their own leaders" (Adams, 1972, p. 497) can be powerful tools for adult educators. As case studies and topics of class discussions, these tools excite students and remind practitioners of their work as adult educators of the community. Action and reflection can be modeled to the fullest extent. The result is that students and organizational clients benefit. As long as I can juggle the logistical details, I will continue to enjoy the best of both worlds.

References

Adams, F. "Highlander Folk School: Getting Information, Going Back and Teaching It." *Harvard Educational Review*, 1972, 42 (4), 497–520.

Boyte, H. C. *The Backyard Revolution*. Philadelphia: Temple University Press, 1980.

Brookfield, S. D. *Adult Learners, Adult Education, and the Community*. New York: Teachers College Press, 1984.

Greenleaf, R. K. *The Servant as Leader*. Peterborough, N.H.: Center for Applied Studies/ Windy Row Press, 1970.

Lemler, J. B., Miller, J., Palmer, P., Poore, B., Turner-Smith, P., Wakefield, J., Wisely, S., and Tyler Scott, K. *Trustee Education Manual*. Indianapolis, Ind.: Lilly Endowment, 1990.

NORMA S. FRIEDMAN *is professor in the Department of Business and Arts, Indiana Institute of Technology, Fort Wayne. In addition to her private consulting practice, she is a trustee educator and consultant with the Trustee Leadership Development Program in Indianapolis.*

*The road to success as a full-time consultant is paved with learning,
practice, and variety.*

Consulting: A Full-Time Job

George B. Thomas

Let me begin with why I work as a consultant. Wanting to have influence
on organizations without having ultimate responsibility for them is certainly high on the list. Twenty years ago, I was an associate dean and
lecturer at the Harvard Graduate School of Education. I had just finished
a doctorate in American intellectual history. I was being groomed to be in
charge of an education institution—a college president, an education
school dean, a headmaster.

I took some time off and looked down deep. I had just gone through
the crucible of the 1960s at a great university. During those years, my
colleagues and I talked a lot about who was running things. I clearly
remember a Students for a Democratic Society map tying all of us power
brokers together. My journal of that pause for self-examination dwells
largely on power: wanting it, having it, using it. At the same time, I was
making my first explorations of management and organizations. Until
then, I had been a singularly uncurious and untaught manager. My work
as a dean at Harvard was completely intuitive. No one sent me to management courses; my mentors were not very effective; I had equally untutored
role models; I had never even heard of administrative theory. So I was
totally unprepared for a sympathetic intervention that made me look at my
management behavior for the first time.

One fall, the Ford Foundation provided a Harvard sabbatical for a
union leader who had been a critical advocate of the New York City
decentralization battles of the mid-1960s. I met this man, who was a rough-
hewn, up-from-the-ranks unionist and plenty smart, on and off the street.
One morning he dropped by my office and asked if he could sit in a corner
and watch me. "Sure," I said.

I proceeded to practice my dean business: fifteen-minute appointments with colleagues and students interrupted by telephone calls and visits from my secretary. At the end of the morning, my visitor took me out to lunch. "Why do you chop up your time that way?" he asked. I had to admit I had no idea, although I suspect, in retrospect, that I was copying my boss. "Well," my visitor said, "my sense is that you didn't deal thoroughly with a single person you saw." From that moment, I became aware of management style.

During my months of self-exploration, I decided that being in charge of an organization was not all that important to me. I could be influential (powerful) in other ways, including consulting, although I had precious little idea of what consulting was.

I did a stint teaching in Boston and saw firsthand the political side of the system as I attended school committee meetings. I began to look carefully at the behavior and motivation of bureaucrats. I attended teachers' meetings that were total top-down farces. I got hooked and left curriculum development for a lifetime of figuring out and consulting in systems.

Learning How to Consult

Eventually, I left deaning to start a small company designed to provide consulting services to schools. Several years of deaning had equipped me for teaching or deaning, not for consulting. I had no training—formal or informal—in any of the skills wanted in the marketplace. In order to make a living, I had to start by learning evaluation techniques and (probably more important) developing skills in marketing, writing reports and proposals, contracting, and running meetings.

What was indispensable was that I did that learning with colleagues. We pooled our meager knowledge and pushed one another to try new things. We mentored one another, and we had the considerably good fortune to have one older partner who was a teacher but who knew some of the moves of a successful consultant.

I cannot imagine starting without colleagues. When people ask me, "How can I become a consultant?" I answer, invariably, "Join a group to learn the ropes. Get some solid group experience, first, before going solo." We were not a perfect group, but we worked hard at our groupness, our marketing, and our visibility.

As the firm grew, I became increasingly responsible for generating work for others, and I liked the hands-on work better. I gradually began to try on more of a consulting role, selling my time directly, by the day, working as a soloist. And that has been my work life for the past fifteen years. At any given time, I am juggling half a dozen projects, some large, some small, and keeping my eyes and ears open for new ones. It always starts simply. Someone says,

"George, we're having a tough time helping two different cultures at the bank understand each other." I answer, "Well, let me show you an instrument and workshop a couple of my colleagues use."

Early on in my consulting career, my father asked me how I spent my time. My father was a very successful, very traditional head of an academic department at an Ivy League university. (He was also a first-rate academic entrepreneur who built a nationally recognized department from scratch, an ability I never fully appreciated when he was living.) After supper one evening, he sat me down. "How are you spending your time, George?" he asked. This was a first. My father generally kept his nose out of my career, although I knew he was disappointed when I left deaning at Harvard for "consulting." (I suspect that he had never talked to a consultant in the flesh.) I carefully explained what any full-time consultant would have explained: juggling half a dozen projects of varying size. For him, the consummate teacher, I added my gloss on the educational content of each assignment. Yes, I was a consultant, but I was an educator of adults at the same time. My father listened patiently. I waited for his response. It came slowly. Finally, he said, with just a touch of exasperation, "George, why don't you just get a job?"

Variety with Some Consistent Themes

My assignments as a consultant have been wildly diverse, from helping the United Nations Children's Fund connect with slum improvement activists in Pakistan to redesigning document handling for the Internal Revenue Service. Some common threads, however, do run through the variety. The main work I do is helping to run meetings (facilitation as opposed to training, writing reports, or coaching). As a facilitator, I need to take into account timing, lighting, seating, flipcharts, ventilation, and other logistical elements. More important, I need to develop a "design" for each meeting, a scenario of the activities that the group wants to undertake. The agenda is the core of the design, and the order of the groupings and regroupings of participants is critical. Invariably, I develop this design with the client, preferably with a "design group" of participants. If it is a single session with a group, I insist on individual interviews, introduce myself, gather expectations, look for potential loose cannons, and prepare for the design phase. Before the session, I ask the whole group to agree on the design, and I make sure to have several checkpoints during the day. I try to stay neutral; but if I want to express my opinion, I announce that I am stepping out of my role as facilitator.

I am an enthusiastic and engaged facilitator. I set and maintain the rhythm of the session as someone sympathetic with the group's purposes. I do a lot of flipchart recording of the main points that participants make and agree on.

I rely heavily on a very few devices: brainstorming, prioritizing, force-fielding, and applying criteria. I encourage consensual decision making. I admire consultants who have lots of handy-dandy process tools in their kit bags, but I usually remember the relevant tools too late to use them. I suspect this is because I use personality and enthusiasm more than formal technique to keep group momentum going.

My real joy derives from the rhythm of helping a group come to a conclusion. The core stuff of most group meetings (indeed, of most consulting work) is opening up the group to produce new ideas and then narrowing down those ideas. Opening up is frequently accomplished by brainstorming or visioning. Narrowing down involves making choices, usually by generating and then applying criteria or by voting processes. The facilitator's task is to find a meeting rhythm that engenders participation, that convinces each participant that her or his ideas are getting a reasonable hearing, even if they do not rise to the top.

I have recently concluded that structured consensus building is at the very heart of the group process skills that facilitators wield. It is a thread that runs clear up to the latest tool: search conferences. We group and regroup people to help them understand what they agree on. For me, there is something magical about finding what we are currently calling "common ground," developing agreement on conclusions that meld together the bits and pieces of individuals' ideas. When an individual participant buys into a group consensus to which he or she only contributed a minuscule portion, that is success.

For the past ten years, the main thrust of my work with nonprofits has been planning. Basically, the planning process I practice is a variant on management by objectives. In the early 1970s, much of the planning I did started with an issue or problem census: an analysis of defects in current operations. My approach was myopic and inwardly turned. I remember a long day at the Boston University School of Education when we papered the wall with problems; clustered, combined, and prioritized them; and ended up with an action plan for dealing with them—not a word of the outside world, or of the future or the past, for that matter.

Since then, the front end of planning has changed. Most organizations look outward at the "environment," often the competition, for trends and external events. Most try to start planning with a vision, a picture of a desired future, compared to the current state. Once the initial stages are accomplished, the main work of developing strategies and crafting an action plan stays pretty much the same.

One highly useful idea has been to add examination of the organization's history and values to the initial stages of the planning. In one variant, adapted by a group funded by the Lilly Endowment from work with midwestern religious congregations, the planning group develops a time line, charting and discussing key events in the organization's history. Not only does this approach provide a valuable context (and a lively, interactive start) for a planning retreat, it also helps ensure that the plans developed will remain rooted in the organization's past, in its culture and traditions.

Suggestions About Consulting

Over the years, I have collected a few suggestions for people thinking of full-time careers in consulting.

Start with an Established Group. The major mystery of consulting is learning what to do for a client, but there are other mysteries: marketing, contracting, controlling time, reporting, and billing. I cannot imagine someone learning all of these skills alone. Consequently, I always advise would-be consultants to join a group (not start a group) and learn how they do consulting work. Apprentice consultants do not have to stay affiliated for a long period or mimic the group's procedures in the long run. But they do need to learn the ropes before starting to walk on them. Then they can leave, but with work under contract to tide them over.

Spread the Income Base. At one point, I was nestled into a three-day-a-week contract with a single client. The contract had been going on for several years. I was gradually taking on more responsibility. I was gradually slowing down my marketing, my exposure, and my availability to other clients. With no warning, I was fired. That started the worst period of my consulting career. I was angry, confused, without work, alone. It took me three or four months to recapture a reasonable amount of work. Now, at any one time, I have half a dozen projects in the pipeline. They vary in size, but they keep me active and exposed.

Diversify. When I left deaning, the group that I cofounded aspired to full-scale organization development work. We concentrated mostly on the evaluation of education programs, evaluation that was required by public and private funding sources. Evaluation funding began to dry up. Gradually, I learned enough research techniques to run a couple of large research projects. Planning came along in the late 1970s, and diversity training later. Five years ago, I affiliated with a group to do work-systems design projects.

At no point have I dropped my willingness to perform any of these earlier activities. Along the way, I have helped design a city and acted as its temporary superintendent of schools, developed slum improvement projects in Pakistan, written a paper on child labor worldwide, helped telephone company employees build teams, and resolved conflicts for half a dozen trustee boards.

In short, I have diversified. I have some experience in most of the kinds of activities that nonprofits ask for, and I am ready to try others.

Request Continual Performance Appraisal. A consultant is a hired helper, an extra brain. Performance assessment is a way of ensuring that the right work is being done at the right pace, for projects of even the shortest duration. After lunch of a one-day retreat with a new client, I will ask, "How did the morning go? Do we need to slow down? Are your expectations being met?" During the five years I consulted with one organization, I tried to have my performance appraised every time I came to work.

I do not wait to be praised or criticized. I initiate the inquiry. Not everyone is willing or able to assess me thoroughly, but, without it, I do not know whether a different approach is needed.

Keep It Simple and Prompt. I am not especially fond of jabber about "being professional." A few things, however, ring true. I always answer all mail and all telephone calls immediately (although I am not quite as fanatic as a colleague for whom everything is "urgent").

I am especially careful to submit reports on time. Clients (should) expect promptness, precision, and cleanliness. As for the rest of professionalism, I do some things and do not do others. I am not, and was never, "George B. Thomas and Associates." (I associate with some colleagues, but they are not my "associates.") I have never had my own brochure. I always carry business cards. I have a fax machine. I have two types of résumés— one "academic," listing all work and reports on five pages, and one "commercial," a single page. I bill quickly and neatly.

Beyond these externals, what is "professionalism"? For me, it is in part the ability to juggle half a dozen projects at one time. I crave the variety; it is a pleasure to move from one arena to another. The downside of being a generalist is that I never practice any one skill or know any one kind of client really well, the way a specialist does. It is hard to keep a conceptual thread running through my work in the same way as a consultant who spends all of his or her time in, for example, overseas development or quality of production methods. However, I learn a lot, a bit of each specialty, and that kind of professional development meets many of my needs.

Half a dozen projects at a time also means careful time discipline. I keep track of my time, not in fifteen-minute increments but usually by half-days. I cannot afford to spend a lot of unbilled time, and so I estimate carefully time commitments in the initial proposal and track them assiduously.

Marketing. My experience with marketing is doubtless idiosyncratic. (Obviously, much of what I do as a consultant is idiosyncratic.) The prevailing wisdom has the consultant getting work via good-looking brochures, published articles, speeches at conferences, and public seminars. I disagree.

My last twenty projects, over roughly three years of work, range from two-day board development sessions to year-long redesign interventions. More than half of the twenty projects came to me (I did not "find" them) through connections first established fifteen years ago with a midwestern foundation. I have produced for the foundation; people whom I have met through that work have touted me to others. I actively solicited only one of the twenty recent projects, and that project led to three more small ones.

The largest money earners came through the Synapse Group, which I helped start five years ago. At that point, I was working mostly with nonprofits and selling time to a company that provided diversity training to telephone companies. Another trainer told me about his long-held aspiration to form a group to specialize in work-systems design. I started the first project, for a big energy company, with almost no warning or preparation. I managed to stay about half an inch ahead of the client for a year.

Since then, I have averaged one work-systems design project a year. They pay double what I can get from nonprofits. And I think they have vastly expanded my understanding of organizations. The six members of the Synapse Group meet three or four times a year to share insights, analyze the clients, and search for new marketing ideas. That collegiality is immensely helpful.

But I have not given up my work for nonprofits. Given my background and values, it is hard to get totally excited about an outfit that sells energy, or another that makes starch from corn. Still, the folks are pretty much the same. Now I know how inappropriate it is to say of a nonprofit, "If only they were more businesslike!"

Collegiality. There has been precious little collegiality in my work for nonprofits, which occupies perhaps one-half of my time and brings in about one-third of my income. I know perhaps twenty full-time consultants who work for nonprofits. Not one of them, in twenty years, has offered to share work with me. I have sent a small amount of work to perhaps six of those twenty people. I suspect this is "normal." We keep the work that we get. Right now, I am riding shotgun for a colleague in a fifteen-month design contract. He and I are almost as intimately involved in every aspect of the project as I was involved with my teaching colleagues in Boston twenty-five years ago.

But that kind of day-in, day-out collegiality is rare for me. More common is the occasional insight. A black male colleague in a diversity workshop pointed out that I wrote male participants' statements on the blackboard without comment and restated women's statements. Another colleague pointed out that brainstormed ideas are clearer and sharper if they are expressed with at least four words. And my understanding of participation was deepened by listening to slum dwellers in Pakistan along with two Indian colleagues. I send the larger circle of twenty colleagues my consulting reports when I am proud of them.

Still, all in all, it is lonely out there: competitive, isolated, and often uncongenial. Periodically, I say to myself, "If I went to organizational development network meetings or taught a course . . ." I reply, "My schedule is just too erratic for such regular connecting." Basically, I think I enjoy the "solo-ness."

Conclusion

What is the best and the worst of full-time consulting? One best is the variety; no one day in my life is like another. That seems to meet a basic drive of mine. Another best is related to my original ideas about consulting: I can have influence on an institution, but I do not have to worry about it night and day. And, despite my father's skepticism, I have spent my life educating adults—and myself.

The worst? There is no security whatsoever. This is the first time in twenty years that I can coast on a relatively secure income for a year because of a long contract. I am envious of some specialists; my speciality is "process," and that feels soft sometimes. Yes, I do miss an institutional setting, the library, the lunches with colleagues, and the feeling of building a place that I shall eventually leave behind. I am proud, however, of surviving well in a competitive environment.

GEORGE B. THOMAS is a consultant and partner in the Synapse Group, Boston.

The consultant as facilitator of the group process can be a compelling force in effecting personal growth and change.

The Consultant as Personal Change Agent

Joan C. Goldberg

In this chapter, I reflect on my role as an adult education consultant. My work focuses on the promotion of personal change through the use of group processes and collaborative learning. I work primarily with women who are coping with life crises or transitions that are dramatically affecting their lives (Schlossberg, Troll, and Leibowitz, 1978; Walz and Benjamin, 1980).

Because their current realities are so completely different from their hopes, dreams, and expectations, these women often experience both internal and external conflict. For example, they might be dealing with care of an aging parent, separation and divorce, death of a spouse, job loss, entering or reentering the job market, or job or career change. They may be trying to cope with their singleness in a couples' world. No matter what issues they are confronting, these women often feel that these particular events have been "forced" on them, that their situations were not their choice—not the way things were "supposed" to be (Sheehy, 1976; Neugarten and Neugarten, 1987). Within this ever-changing society, they are particularly vulnerable, as there is not an effective support structure to serve as a buffer throughout the transition process.

My Role as Personal Change Agent

My own transition experiences were the catalyst for my desire to create a "safe" environment where women can gather to learn from and connect with one another, to consider alternative ways of thinking and being, and to identify needed resources and services. Diverse learning formats char-

NEW DIRECTIONS FOR ADULT AND CONTINUING EDUCATION, no. 58, Summer 1993 © Jossey-Bass Publishers

acterize my practice. They can take the form of a noncredit continuing education course, a support group, in-service training, a workplace seminar, or a more intensive ongoing program. The settings and times in which I practice are equally diverse and include urban, suburban, and rural areas, daytime, evening, and weekend hours. Church basements, community centers, schools, senior centers, town halls, and senior residences have been my "offices" and "classrooms." Of course, where and how I work depends on my clients' needs, schedules, and budgets as well as their motivation and availability.

Equally important in my diversified practice is the freedom and flexibility to create and design my own programs—those that I feel are most appropriate to the women I serve. As a consultant, I have the autonomy to maintain control over all of the components of the program. Even when my client is an agency that takes responsibility for publicity, outreach, and recruitment and, at times, may even determine the program content, I remain involved in the planning and contribute my network and contacts, ideas, and experience and expertise. In this way, I am an integral part of the process. Because of this attention to client need, each combination of program, location, time, and medium has proved to be a powerful catalyst, stimulating the participants' insight, growth, and awareness of their capacity to make changes in their lives.

While the flexibility and independence of my consulting practice offer great advantages in meeting the needs of women in transition, the task of reaching those who could most benefit from my services is a challenge, requiring continuous marketing and selling of my skills and program ideas. This effort involves building and maintaining a network of contacts, being aware of current trends and needs, and finding the right vehicle to offer the appropriate program.

In addition to the challenge of marketing and pairing my skills with the identified need, there are significant additional barriers to meeting my clients' needs. These are the women's internal barriers. I often find that although someone is experiencing feelings (often overwhelming) of confusion, uncertainty, or anxiety, she is resistant and reluctant to participate in my programs. Perhaps she is fearful of replicating an earlier, unsatisfactory educational experience and lacks confidence in her own abilities. It may be the unknown quality of a group experience or the admission that she cannot handle the situation alone, thus the risk of exposing weakness and vulnerability, or it may be that she does not want to burden others with her own problems. However, attempts to deal with a situation "alone" only create additional stress and anxiety, and possibly even depression, heightening the sense of a loss of control over one's life. The constant challenge for me, therefore, is to increase a program's accessibility by trying to eliminate these internal as well as external barriers (Darkenwald and Larson, 1980). Strategies that seem to be effective in dealing with this challenge start with the practical aspects of my clients' lives. For example, since family caregivers may not be able to attend a workshop or support group because of the time of day, the location, or their inability to leave the family members in their care, I may arrange to use senior center facilities for a morning workshop. Recently, the manager of a newly opened senior residence offered me use of the facility and volunteered to provide transportation, if needed, as well as on-site care for any elderly family members. This agreement was mutually beneficial. It gave caregivers the chance to easily participate in the group and the care recipients the opportunity for outside social contact. It also enhanced the image of the residence in the community.

Another strategy that I use to deal with the internal barriers involves question-format advertisements that capture attention and appeal to the need to solve a specific problem (Edwards and Edwards, 1991). For example, one advertisement that I developed for a family caregivers group read, "Caring for an aging family member? Feeling guilty and overwhelmed?" Feedback from this effort was very positive: "The words jumped out at me." "This is just what I have been looking for." "I've been thinking about this for years and suddenly this seems like the right time."

My Role as Consultant

My role as a consultant enables me to create informal opportunities (both institutional and noninstitutional) to bring groups together around issues central to their lives, to respond to their particular needs and interests, and to provide them with a time and place for themselves where they can come to "talk through their thoughts" and to learn collectively. As I prepared to write this chapter, I reread evaluations of past participants and talked with former students. One woman had written, "I felt a definite bonding grow during the course of the program. There was a lot of personal growth going on. The instructor had a lot to do with it." In rereading these evaluations, I was able to clarify my thoughts about my role in making this process work.

The participants suggested that my openness, honesty, and model of self-disclosure encouraged them to become actively involved in the programs. They experienced me as affirming, understanding, empathic, caring, and not afraid to reveal my own vulnerability and my own needs. It was clear to me that I was someone they could relate to and whom they felt understood them. "This is not a good-bye letter," one participant had written me. "You cannot just dismiss someone who has been a friend, teacher, and role model; at least I can't."

As a consultant, I share not only my personal self with them but also my knowledge and skills. All the while I encourage their expertise. They are my peers and my teachers as well. They come to the learning groups with their own experiences and backgrounds, motivated to satisfy existing needs and achieve immediate goals (Houle, 1972). Since they are the resources, the "experts" diagnosing their own needs and no longer the empty vessels waiting to be filled, my role as instructor becomes demystified (Freire, 1970). I try to maintain a delicate balance between being part of the group and providing information, resources, and support; a balance between attending to the needs of the participants and presenting content. Utilizing my own expertise and the expertise of guest speakers and outside resources, I provide the information that they are seeking and link them to resources in the community, and thus I assist them in developing their own support networks.

As a facilitator, I must be responsive to the needs of the group, flexible to deal with unscheduled issues, and willing to "let go" of my carefully planned agenda as participants bring issues with them that interfere with the process. For example, in one case I was facilitating a stress management workshop for the clerical staff of a local company. As they talked about their expectations for the workshop, I heard a lot of resistance and some real anger and resentment expressed about the company requirement to attend this workshop. Rather than compulsively pursue my own schedule, I made an on-the-spot decision to give them permission to voice their concerns. Only then was I successfully able to relate their experience back to the topic of stress. In their evaluations, participants commented on the value of that discussion. For them, it was the most valuable part of the workshop. I realized that I had provided a unique opportunity for them just to talk with one another about some of their immediate feelings and concerns, an opportunity that the work setting did not in general offer them in any structured way. I also realized that had I not initially set aside my original plan, I would have lost the group and the results would have been disastrous.

Process

For the first session of a group, I begin by sharing something about myself, who I am, and an example of my own experience. Depending on the topic, I might relate some of my struggles in coping with an aging father, living on my own, developing a more positive sense of myself, or creating my own business. Then, one by one, the group members have the opportunity to tell their stories, why they came, and their expectations. My model encourages them to share feelings and invites their participation. The atmosphere is casual, relaxed, informal, private. We agree to respect the confidentiality of the group. I emphasize that this is not group therapy, but it can be an opportunity for participants to increase their self-awareness and enhance their personal effectiveness (Ironside and Jacobs, 1977).

I present a suggested agenda, which is modified as participants' expectations and needs are incorporated into the content. I share specific information that, along with readings and other materials, helps clarify central issues, always relating it back to their own experiences, their own lives. There is always time for their personal responses and reactions, for them to interact and become involved with one another. As the process unfolds, as they hear others echo what they each have been feeling and thinking, I observe the smiles and nods of recognition, of insight, and of shared understandings. I witness the instant disclosure of feelings and thoughts, the mutual support and caring that emerges and the trust that grows.

"Once you've heard someone else tell an experience that is like yours, it exerts an irresistible pull" (Steinem, 1992, p. 26). They may talk about a range of issues: about the guilt they feel as daughters of aging parents, the need for time for themselves, the stresses and strains of trying to juggle work and family responsibilities, the loneliness of being recently divorced, or the lack of confidence as one contemplates a return to the workplace after many years at home. In group after group, I have repeatedly heard many of the same themes—each participant thinking that she was the only one. Repeatedly, I am struck by the openness, honesty, and humor that seem to sustain them. The group listens, expressing understanding and empathy, not shock and horror, at the feelings expressed so openly.

Because, in most instances, the participants come of their own volition and with expressed needs, they are active learners, and their needs determine much of the content of the sessions (Knowles, 1980). I watch the transformation that emerges from the comfort of a group that is united by sharing similar feelings, problems, and experiences (Mezirow, 1978). When they allow themselves to explore options and alternatives, they find new ways to deal with their situations and form their own support networks. Through collaborative exploration, they find collective solutions. By affirming others and being affirmed by them, they enhance their awareness of themselves, their ability to connect and interact with others, and their own self-worth.

Obviously, the process does not work for everyone. There is resistance if one does not choose but rather is required to participate. The group may be a disappointment if one comes with the expectation of a traditional formal learning situation, a "class," offering very specific information without participation.

Results

Through sharing of perceptions and ideas, giving and receiving, helping one another and supporting one another's growth, group participants become a community. They receive the practical information that they came for, connecting not only with one another but also with an array of services and resources. They become more open to new ideas and information. They develop the confidence and courage to begin to address decisions and to take risks. They are more hopeful and aware that they have more possibilities than they once thought. All this happens in an environment in which the group functions as a source of learning and change and as a powerful agent for personal growth.

Reflections

Long after the programs are completed, the words of the participants remain. "Thank you for empowering those of us who are hesitant." They have taught me about the importance of women's relationships with other women and the individual change, learning, and growth that result from these connections. They have reinforced my belief in the potential of the group process as an element in personal change. For the clients, increased self-awareness leads them to greater control over their lives and empowers them to take responsibility. "It has given me the push to go ahead with what I knew I had to do [placement of a parent in a nursing home], now knowing it's my only alternative."

I have been privileged to witness, as well as be a part of, the enormous power, courage, and humor that these women possess. I have seen how the bonds form among women. Those bonds often endure long after the group has disbanded formally. When groups continue to meet on their own, I always make myself available to them as a resource. As I participate in the change that occurs in their inner worlds, I am aware of their collective strength to change their outer worlds as well.

References

Darkenwald, G. G., and Larson, G. A. (eds.). *Reaching Hard-to-Reach Adults.* New Directions for Adult and Continuing Education, no. 8. San Francisco: Jossey-Bass, 1980.

Edwards, P., and Edwards, S. *Getting Business to Come to You.* Los Angeles: Tarcher, 1991.

Freire, P. *Pedagogy of the Oppressed.* New York: Continuum, 1970.

Houle, C. O. *The Design of Education.* San Francisco: Jossey-Bass, 1972.

Ironside, D. J., and Jacobs, D. E. *Trends in Counseling and Information Services for the Adult Learner.* Toronto: Ontario Institute for Studies in Education, 1977.

Knowles, M. S. *Modern Practice of Adult Education.* (Rev. ed.) Chicago: Follett, 1980.

Mezirow, J. *Education for Perspective Transformation.* New York: Center for Adult Education, Teachers College, Columbia University, 1978.

Neugarten, B. L., and Neugarten, D. A. "The Changing Meanings of Age." *Psychology Today,* May 1987, pp. 29–32.

Schlossberg, N. K., Troll, L. E., and Liebowitz, Z. *Perspectives on Counseling Adults: Issues and Skills.* Pacific Grove, Calif.: Brooks/Cole, 1978.

Sheehy, G. *Passages: Predictable Crises of Adult Life.* New York: Dutton, 1976.

Steinem, G. "Helping Ourselves to Revolution." *Ms.,* 1992, 3 (3), 24–29.

Walz, G. R., and Benjamin, L. *Counseling Adults for Life Transitions.* Ann Arbor, Mich.: ERIC/ Counseling and Personnel Services, 1980.

JOAN C. GOLDBERG *is an adult education counselor and consultant, and adjunct instructor at Onondaga Community College, in Syracuse, New York.*

Effective organizational change requires consultants who can create trusting relationships and learning communities.

The Consultant as Organizational Change Agent

Gayle Moller

Consultants assist organizations in designing, implementing, and evaluating major organizational change efforts in turbulent environments. The difficulty of the process is compounded when an organization has many layers of decision makers who exhibit varying degrees of resistance to change and reluctance to deal with demands placed on the organization. The task of the consultant then becomes one of weaving a web of positive relationships within the organization. In order to weave this web, the consultant must understand the social structure of the organization and how people interact within that structure and delve beneath the surface level of the organization to the assumptions and "psyche" of the group (Mitroff, 1983).

When I describe my work as a change agent, I conjure up images of a weblike diagram showing how each organizational component links to another. Of course, this is disturbing to those who are looking for linear relationships. Since most of the work is intuitive (Schön, 1987), there is a guiding vision that is difficult to explain to colleagues. "What do I do for a living?" I am asked. The answer is that I link relationships to build learning communities in order to effect change.

Context of Organizational Change

The context of my work is public education systems in five metropolitan school districts, which include over 625 schools. Although these are unique public sector organizations, their struggles appear similar to those described in the literature for other types of organizations, as many enterprises are being challenged to rethink their approaches to doing business.

The public, as well as professionals in education, have acknowledged the need for significant changes in schools. The changes demanded are not incremental but transformational. This type of change requires the organizational members to move outside their present paradigms, or ways of thinking, to new visions of how business can be accomplished (Burns, 1978; Tichy and Devanna, 1986). One could compare this transformation to world events of the last few years. How many of us were ready for the Berlin Wall to come down? Or for the former Soviet Union to change so dramatically? School systems are on the brink of similarly significant change.

Transformational changes are "second-order" changes, which "shift the system irreversibly to a new and revolutionary paradigm" (Dunphy and Stace, 1988, p. 323). In contrast, previous school reforms are examples of "first-order" changes, which do not disturb the basic structure of the organization (Bartunek, 1984; Levy, 1986). First-order changes assume that the structure is adequate and what we need to do is correct the way in which policies are implemented. For instance, if students are not learning how to calculate, we must increase the number of drills for students in the basic skills. Deal (1990, p. 9) believes that "schools will become fundamentally different only when we quit correcting surface deficiencies and recognize that transformation involves a collective re-negotiation of historically anchored myths, metaphors, and meaning."

Change takes place within what Weick (1976) labeled "loosely coupled relationships." Schools are connected to a larger organization but maintain their own identities. Similarly, teachers are part of an individual school, but they also work independently. Educators are being asked to change schools; yet transformation in these loosely coupled organizations is difficult when everyone has gone through the system as a student. The influential members of the public and professional educators perceive their past schooling experiences as successful. School personnel are being challenged to change schools in an environment of *both* criticism of their effectiveness and a desire to maintain the status quo.

Client Characteristics

School systems are hierarchical in structure. The consultant works with three levels when working through an organizational change effort. The first is the top level, which includes school board members, superintendents, and deputy and associate superintendents. In the middle are the individuals with line authority between the schools and the top-level managers. Finally, the school site involves the principal and other faculty and staff. Within this structure there are obstacles in the system that prevent its transformation (Senge, 1990).

Top-Level Managers: Accepting an Alien System. Individual schools are functioning within an existing system while attempting to introduce change through a new and "alien" system. McLaughlin and Marsh (1978) identified institutional motivation for change as a critical factor in a successful project. The very reasons that an organization becomes involved in a change effort affect the success of the project. In order for the change to be effective, the participants must perceive that the larger school system and top-level managers are ready for and support the new, alien system.

Just as individuals seek opportunities to learn when a significant transition occurs, organizations also seek change in response to a crisis (Bartunek, 1984; Bedeian, 1986). If an organization is comfortable with the existing system, it is difficult to change (Nurick, 1985). As Beer (1987, p. 27) has stated, "Starting a transformation in advance of a crisis and without enough top management consensus about impending problems . . . raises the likelihood that it will become just another program."

It is also true that contradictions exist in many school systems. Although there is an espoused concern about a crisis in the school system, top-level members' behaviors support the existing system. There may be a noncrisis attitude while the top-level leaders within a school system announce there is a crisis. If a crisis is acknowledged, and yet the behavior of management leads others to believe that the existing system is functioning satisfactorily, how can change occur? The lack of congruence between the existing system and the new system may inhibit the change effort (Lawler, 1986; Stein and Kanter, 1980; Walton, 1985). These types of clients present a challenge to the consultant.

Middle Managers: Caught in the Middle. When a school district implements a new system within an existing system, there may be confusion. The present system is a structure that relies on hierarchical authority to establish policies and procedures. School-level personnel are accountable to the middle managers. A new system may allow school staffs to move past this layer of line authority to appeal directly to top management for changes in the policies and procedures. Middle managers are caught between supporting the existing systems and encouraging the schools to implement change.

Gilberg (1988) considered the lack of organizational support and the fear of reprisals as barriers to change. Even if the top managers have espoused support for the change, the middle managers have the "problems of interpretation" (Gordon, 1984, p. 177). Day-to-day operations continue and the new system intrudes, while decisions have to be made quickly within the existing system. The dilemmas of middle managers are difficult and force them to fall back on the use of authority to make decisions.

School Personnel: Perceived Obstacles to Change. Changes within organizations are also restricted by a belief among personnel that boundaries are established by top or middle management. Sometimes the boundaries are perceived but not real. School personnel have difficulty discerning formal policy from restrictions assumed but not written. This is an example of distorted communication within the organization (Watkins, 1986). If knowledge is considered power, the distortion of knowledge results in an inequality in the relationships between the people who know—the top-level or middle-level administrators—and the people who think they know, the school personnel.

Administrative control, whether implicit or explicit, endures through the lack of clarity in communication about the boundaries within which people are permitted to make decisions. A self-fulfilling prophecy tends to develop when implicit power is perceived as fact (Gordon, 1984). This results in exaggerated perceptions of the extent of power of top-level and middle-level managers.

The school site itself is where change occurs (Barth, 1990). If school personnel perceive obstacles but those obstacles do not exist, then the role of the consultant is to help these individuals examine their perceptions. My work in the school districts began with these clients, with the support of top and middle management.

Strategies for Linking Relationships

The relationships among the clients within an organization are both defined and undefined. As a consultant in this environment, an understanding of these relationships is crucial. Where are the connections? Where does the consultant start? In my work, I have approached the linking of positive relationships through the strategy of establishing a variety of learning communities.

Organizational change occurs one individual at a time, until a critical mass develops. My work begins with the "believers" and their ability to influence the "nonbelievers." The deficit model of viewing the professional educator as an individual who "needs fixing" has proved to be ineffective. This model has focused on the expert who diagnoses and recommends changes (Sarason, 1982; Sirotnik, 1989). The type of change necessary for reform in schools demands a significant shift in paradigms. The people who will influence change are the participants in the system.

Approaches to linking the relationships among clients for building learning communities are formal and informal. Formal strategies include training and various types of communication vehicles. Informal strategies involve the linkage of people. In addition, measurement of our success as consultants is now thought of in terms of outcomes for our clients.

Formal Strategies. Participants are invited to attend a multiday retreat where everyone is requested to stay on location. During the sessions, there is a mixture of learning activities, reflection through writing, and celebration. This retreat is followed by additional learning experiences scheduled over several months. Each session is designed to provide a trusting environment that encourages participants to share their concerns about the change being implemented.

Learning activities encourage participants to take responsibility for the facilitation of learning. Trainers present ideas and resources. Then, the participants organize the learning for others. The synergy inherent to this type of experience demonstrates the value of staying out of the way of the learners and allowing them to take authority for their own learning. This design does not preclude organization of the learning experience. The trainers are responsible for providing the framework in which the learning takes place.

Reflection in journals has become a mainstay in the design of training. Participants are introduced to journal writing through an assigned free-writing experience. The trainer explains the value of reflection and then invites the participants to write continuously for a defined period of time. Usually seven to ten minutes provide an adequate amount of time for the writing period. While the participants are writing, the trainers write. Assigned free writing is used only on the first day. The trainers respond to the journal entries nightly. This strategy has resulted in a deep level of writing from the participants as compared to simply inviting them to write in a journal. The next morning, after responding to the journals, the trainers get together and identify the common themes that appeared in the journals they read. Confidentiality is maintained, but ideas from the journals are shared with the participants before beginning the next session.

Celebrations are a key component in my programs. All schedules include time for fun. Photographs of these activities serve to link sessions. Humor is considered a primary learning tool in the design of the learning experiences. Participants in the sessions are from different levels of school systems, and these opportunities encourage a feeling of peer equity among the group.

Informal Strategies. By understanding relationships within organizations, consultants can use several informal strategies to link positive relationships among clients. One strategy is to develop a sociogram of the relationships within the particular school system. Influential people within the system are linked to the individuals who are actively involved in the learning experiences developed by the consultant. If the learning experiences are successful, the participants become ambassadors for the change effort. The role of the consultant is to understand the relationships and develop strategies to link individuals. Often, top and middle managers, although caught up in the existing system, will respond to bottom-up recommendations from influential school personnel. Regardless of the vehicle used, the consultant's aim is to keep the change effort visible to the clients. Once clients have a successful learning experience, the strategies that follow are usually successful. One follow-up strategy is the use of informal notes or postcards, rather than formal correspondence, to communicate support of the change effort. This type of correspondence gets the attention of the recipient. Telephone calls, visits to sites, and newsletters can also be used toward this end.

Conclusion

The consultant can assume that obstacles will challenge any change effort. Top-level managers may proclaim support of a change effort yet exhibit behaviors that support business as usual. Middle managers may have difficulty determining whether to support the new system or to try to maintain balance in the existing system. School personnel may misinterpret communications and perceive obstacles that do not exist.

Organizational change depends on linking positive relationships to form learning communities that promote the change effort and seek to overcome the obstacles. The consultant serves as a catalyst in the process of linking the relationships through formal and informal strategies. Rather than depend on a deficit model, the consultant involves the learners in the task of designing their own future.

Schools, and other organizations, are dependent on the people within their systems to influence the change process. The consultant's role is to work with supportive top and middle managers to develop an environment that encourages risk taking and addresses the transformational change needed for improved education.

References

Barth, R. S. *Improving Schools from Within: Teachers, Parents, and Principals Can Make the Difference.* San Francisco: Jossey-Bass, 1990.

Bartunek, J. M. "Changing Interpretive Schemes and Organizational Restructuring." *Administrative Science Quarterly,* 1984, *29,* 355–372.

Bedeian, A. G. "Contemporary Challenges in the Study of Organizations." *Journal of Management,* 1986, *12,* 185–201.

Beer, M. "The Critical Path for Change: Keys to Success and Failure in Six Companies." In R. H. Kilmann, T. J. Covin, and Associates, *Corporate Transformation: Revitalizing Organizations for a Competitive World.* San Francisco: Jossey-Bass, 1987.

Burns, J. M. *Leadership.* New York: HarperCollins, 1978.

Deal, T. E. "Reframing Reform." *Educational Leadership,* 1990, *71* (9), 6–12.

Dunphy, D. C., and Stace, D. A. "Transformational and Coercive Strategies for Planned Organization Change: Beyond the O.D. Model." *Organizational Studies,* 1988, *9,* 317–334.

Gilberg, J. "Managerial Attitudes Toward Participative Management Programs: Myths and Reality." *Public Personnel Management,* 1988, *17,* 109–123.

Gordon, D. *The Myths of School Self-Renewal.* New York: Teachers College Press, 1984.

Lawler, E. E., III. *High-Involvement Management: Participative Strategies for Improving Organizational Performance.* San Francisco: Jossey-Bass, 1986.

Levy, A. "Second-Order Planned Change: Definition and Conceptualization." *Organizational Dynamics,* 1986, *15* (1), 5–20.

McLaughlin, M. W., and Marsh, D. D. "Staff Development and School Change." *Teachers College Record*, 1978, *80*, 69–94.

Mitroff, I. I. "Archetypal Social Systems Analysis: On the Deeper Structure of Human Systems." *Academy of Management Review*, 1983, *8*, 387–397.

Nurick, A.J.P. "The Paradox of Participation: Lessons from the TVA." *Human Resource Management*, 1985, *24*, 341–356.

Sarason, S. *The Culture of the School and the Problem of Change*. Needham Heights, Mass.: Allyn & Bacon, 1982.

Schön, D. A. *Educating the Reflective Practitioner: Toward a New Design for Teaching and Learning in the Professions*. San Francisco: Jossey-Bass, 1987.

Senge, P. M. *The Fifth Discipline: The Art and Practice of the Learning Organization*. New York: Doubleday, 1990.

Sirotnik, K. A. "The School as the Center of Change." In T. Sergiovanni and J. H. Moore (eds.), *School for Tomorrow: Directing Reforms to Issues that Count*. Needham Heights, Mass.: Allyn & Bacon, 1989.

Stein, B., and Kanter, R. M. "Building a Parallel Organization." *Journal of Applied Behavioral Science*, 1980, *16* (3), 371–388.

Tichy, N. M., and Devanna, M. A. *The Transformational Leader*. New York: Wiley, 1986.

Walton, R. E. "From Control to Commitment in the Workplace." *Harvard Business Review*, 1985, *85* (2), 76–84.

Watkins, P. "From Managerialism to Communicative Competence: Control and Consensus in Educational Administration." *Journal of Educational Administration*, 1986, *24* (1), 86–106.

Weick, K. "Educational Organizations as Loosely Coupled Systems." *Administrative Science Quarterly*, 1976, *21*, 1–19.

GAYLE MOLLER *is executive director of the South Florida Management Development Network in Miami.*

*Strategies and dilemmas of adult education consultants who use
action technologies to build learning organizations are outlined
and illustrated.*

Sculpting the Learning Organization:
Consulting Using Action Technologies

Karen E. Watkins, Victoria J. Marsick

The idea of the learning organization has energized people in many organizations. Many definitions of this idea exist; the most popular is that of
Senge (1990), who identifies five core disciplines: systems thinking, personal mastery, mental models, shared vision, and team learning. Experiments and exemplars also exist, though they are few in number: for
example, Johnsonville Foods (Honold, 1991) and Granite Rock (Case,
1992). However, there are no formulas or time-tested blueprints for the
creation of a learning organization.

For over six years, we have been talking and working with people who
are trying to create learning organizations, writing about the concept and
seeking to identify what organizations need to do to build them. In this
chapter, we outline the nature of the learning organization and describe the
way in which action technologies can be used to build learning organizations. We then outline the strategies and dilemmas of consultants who use
this approach to help build learning organizations.

What Is a Learning Organization?

A learning organization is an organization that has embedded a continuous
learning process within its structure and that has an enhanced organizational capacity to change or transform. Learning is a continuous, strategically used process, integrated with and running parallel to work, that
changes the perceptions, behaviors, beliefs, mental models or paradigms,
strategies, policies, and procedures of people and organizations (Watkins

and Marsick, in press). Each learning organization is unique. However, in general, they share features such as the following:

Leaders who model calculated risk taking and experimentation
Decentralized decision making and employee empowerment
Skills inventories and audits of learning capacity
Systems for sharing learning and using that learning in the business
Rewards and structures for employee initiative
Consideration of long-term consequences and impact on others' work
Frequent use of cross-functional work teams
Opportunities to learn from experience on a daily basis
Culture of feedback and disclosure

There are many possible entry points for a consultant to create a learning organization. The consultant must, however, address two levels of change simultaneously to get results: (1) enhancement of the capacities of individuals to learn, including the development of an organizational culture that supports continuous learning, and (2) development of systems for organizational learning, including a structure that captures learning outcomes and allows them to be used to change organizational ways of working. We have found that three action technologies allow intervention at both of these levels simultaneously: action research, action-reflection learning, and action science.

Using Action Technologies

Action research is the mother of the other two action technologies. All three technologies involve individuals in a joint problem-solving process that requires analysis of the organizational system as a whole, as well as enhancement of individual learning skills within it. In action research, people use data to inform action. In action-reflection learning, people learn how to learn from their experience so that they can act more effectively. And, in action science, people examine their experiences to see patterns of learning or metalearning. In all cases, these insights lead people and organizations to design action in new ways.

Action Research. Action research grew out of the belief that people would take more effective action if they collected and analyzed data together. Kurt Lewin created a process in which people see the need for change as they collect data around a problem, feed it back to the organization, and decide on solutions. This "unfreezes" their understanding and helps them learn. Action research typically involves (1) formation of groups among those who have problems, (2) reflection on problems in groups, (3) collection of data around the problems, (4) group analysis and group feedback, and (5) group-designed interventions to attempt to solve the problems.

Action research, then, is an iterative process of intervention, collection of data on the effectiveness of the intervention, reflection on results, and design of new interventions.

Action-Reflection Learning. Revans (1980) found that people learn best through work in "sets," which strongly resemble action research teams. There is as much emphasis on the use of teams for learning as on the task itself. People solve real problems in real contexts. Problems must be meaningful, which typically means that they are challenging work assignments. Success or failure is highly visible. Group reflection is also a hallmark of this technology (Marsick, Cederholm, Turner, and Pearson, 1992). People do not typically ask questions that challenge their assumptions. Action-reflection learning teams add an element of "strangerness" to heighten the team's ability to probe below the surface with penetrating questions. Teams do not include experts who tell the problem holder what to do because this prevents discovery learning and may not lead to fresh solutions. The nonexpert can ask "dumb questions," which often lead to new insights. Teams may also work on problems for departments and organizations of which they are not a part, and of which they have little prior knowledge.

Action Science. Action science adds to each of the above the idea that we can have a science of interpersonal action (Argyris and Schön, 1974, 1978). Action research focuses on solving a problem; action-reflection learning on learning how to learn while we act; and action science on the reasons why we do not actually do what we say we do. Action science begins with the belief that no one deliberately sets out to make mistakes, yet we often find that we cannot create the solutions we envision. We get stuck, often habitually, yet we cannot see what we are doing wrong or how to change our behavior. Our behaviors are learned, highly skillful responses, many of which are not highly conscious. In action science, we identify predictable patterns in human interaction that lead us to error, and then we learn to change our behaviors to get the results we want. Action science helps people see their behaviors from a systems view, that is, how their actions are shaped by culture and organizational expectations.

Differences Among Action Technologies. The following example illustrates how these three approaches differ. Suppose that a company wanted to use action technologies to implement a shift to Total Quality Management. Through action research, they might form teams of customers and suppliers who would collect data about their relationship and interaction, which could then be used by all parties concerned to redesign the way in which they work together. Through action-reflection learning, they might form teams of managers who needed to learn how to lead differently in a quality culture. These teams might identify challenges such as the new role of a quality leader or the transition to self-directed work teams. Working together on this problem over time, they would also learn and apply quality tools, learn to think and work in a quality culture, tackle problems in the system that interfere with quality, and learn how to learn. Through action science, managers might further analyze why they cannot produce the quality leadership behaviors that they now espouse. They would examine their own experience, identify dysfunctional actions, redesign their interactions, and role-play to acquire new skills in producing these new behaviors. Action science develops norms that support inquiry.

Building a Learning Organization
Through Action Technologies

Earlier, we noted two criteria for a learning organization: (1) the capacities of individuals to learn are enhanced, including an organizational culture that supports continuous learning, and (2) systems for organizational learning are developed, including a structure that captures and uses learning outcomes. Action technologies address the first criterion by enabling members to both solve problems and learn. The solving of problems gives people power over their work lives. Learning allows people to become conscious of what they can transfer to other situations that they face. Teams of people confront the organization when it interferes with learning and change. People develop new skill in challenging mental models and assumptions. Action technologies address the second criterion by creating learning communities in which people experiment with changes, based on their learning, in policies, procedures, and cultural norms. Teams and networks grow that have developed a habit of sharing and acting on information.

To illustrate, one group at a city utility tells the story of a manager who "ordered" the purchasing department to buy new, smaller foreign trucks for repair persons. This move was intended to cut fuel costs. The smaller trucks arrived, and the huge metal boxes that had been custom-designed to carry all of the repair persons' tools were lifted and dropped into the beds of the trucks. But the beds of the new trucks were too small. So, the boxes had to be custom-made again. Had the repair persons been part of the decision-making process in the first place, it seems likely that much more money would have been saved. Decisions such as these are addressed in action groups from many points of view. The utility department might have continued to seek vehicles with lower fuel consumption for ecological reasons, but with the additional stipulation that the truckbeds be large enough to hold the toolboxes. Even a large truck can be retooled to use natural gas. The truck would get more miles per gallon and run virtually clean. The action technologies discussed in this chapter not only help people solve problems such as these but also lead them to ask how organizations can make poor decisions and what systems can be put into place to prevent poor decisions in the future.

Structures must change if learning organizations are to be created, but at the heart of change are people. Johnsonville Foods decided to build people who would then build the organization, not vice versa (Honold, 1991). People in action groups change complex social systems bit by bit as they tackle specific problems that cannot be solved without chipping away at structures, policies, procedures, and cultures. Learning organizations endure because people and systems change. As more people learn to work differently, the shape of the entire organization evolves. People borrow the tools of the scientist and the change agent, experimenting with possibilities and testing for the best solutions.

Not all action teams learn. A colleague who works in a multinational chemical company describes the cookbook way in which quality action teams have been created and misused. Teams go through the motions of meeting, researching issues, and making recommendations, but management has not thought about why and when to use these teams, nor are most of the teams encouraged to do any serious problem solving. The most important learning of team members is that employee involvement is not taken seriously, and that teams are a waste of valuable time.

Implications for Consultants

Consulting on action technologies to build learning organizations requires consultants to be visionaries who lead the way to new understandings of old concepts and strategies. This goal implies transformative learning (Mezirow, 1991), which asks people to make fundamental shifts in thinking. Consultants must also "walk the talk," that is, they must model the new roles and skills that they advocate for their clients.

Transformative Learning. First, the learning organization is a new idea, but the strategies used to build it are not, as is also the case for action technologies. Critics might say that the ideas involved are simply repackaged. However, the repackaging constitutes, in itself, a fundamental shift in the way in which organizations are understood. The strategies must be reinterpreted in the light of new realities.

Action technologies grew out of efforts in the 1940s directed toward planned, participatory change during the industrial era. Organizations, typified as machines, thrived on hierarchy, bureaucracy, and command and control. Savage (1990) has described the current shift in the knowledge era toward a networked organizational structure in which people work together in integrated systems. Work is conceptualized as a process that spans different functions rather than as a product or service passed on in serial fashion from one department to the next. Organizations want to satisfy customers, both internal and external, and thus build in frequent feedback loops that demand continuous learning for continuous improvement. Because employees at all levels are responsible for satisfying customers, empowerment and participation take on new dimensions. Many people, however, resist these changes. They grew up in old-style organizations and need a transformation in the mental models by which they view their work and world in order to understand the learning organization. Consultants find themselves in the role of visionaries. They describe a new world using old terms that no longer carry the same meaning. The consultant helps people to develop new mental models or ways of interpreting their worlds.

For example, consultants ask people to consider the notion that systems (teams, networks, departments, and entire organizations) can learn rather than to think of learning only in terms of individual growth. Learning must be understood outside of the classroom; people learn from their experience informally and collectively (Marsick and Watkins, 1990). This redefinition often causes initial confusion because people are accustomed to equating learning with structured classroom activities for individuals. Managers can account for training results, if only through classroom activities and after-class evaluations. It is harder to measure results when learning is self-initiated, ongoing, and variable because it is not standardized for everyone; or when it takes place through action groups with outcomes measurable for the team, not just individuals.

The word *feedback* also takes on new meaning in the learning organization. In hierarchical organizations, feedback is limited to what the culture tolerates. As Argyris and Schön (1974, 1978) pointed out, there are many "undiscussables" in these organizations, often governed by status, hierarchy, and unexamined beliefs and values. Because people only bring part of themselves to any discussion, solutions are founded on partial truths to which people are not fully committed. Action technologies bring new models for inquiry that help people jointly examine a problem from many diverse perspectives and that delve into matters that people typically hold back. Consultants help teams examine gaps between what they espouse and what they do, challenge their own thinking and that of others without damaging people's feelings, and develop new cultural norms that allow people to learn from mistakes without fear of punishment.

How do consultants use action technologies in their work with organizations? First, they contract with the organization to work on its problems by forming action teams who are empowered to make the changes deemed necessary to solve the problems identified. This empowerment is extremely critical. With the responsibility to solve the problem, but little authority, action teams cannot really take action. The consultant must create a climate in which members of the teams learn enough about how their thinking will be challenged and their emotions engaged throughout this process to decide whether they really want to work on the teams. This climate of inquiry can be created through an overview workshop introducing and demonstrating the action technology. Without voluntary partici-

pation based on informed consent, the interpersonal threat posed by transformational learning can overwhelm the participants and therefore undermine the process.

Once the teams are well formed, training continues to introduce
members to the action process: selecting a problem, determining how to
research it, collecting the data, analyzing the data, redefining the problem,
and creating action experiments to solve or address the problem while
simultaneously creating a way to measure the effectiveness of the action
experiment. The cycle repeats itself until the problem is solved. Training
is needed for each step of the process as well as ongoing training in group
dynamics.

Pride teams at Johnsonville Foods, for example, evolved from simple
problems such as the food in the vending machines to complex structural
problems. The process of working on problems creates new capacities that
in turn can be used to eliminate organizational barriers to learning and
changing. In this way, the action teams create a continuously improving
work force while continuously improving the organization.

Walking the Talk. Action technologies involve new roles for managers
and human resources developers as teachers, consultants, and coaches.
The action technologist models learning and asks that clients do the same
so that everyone within the organization can continuously learn. The
consultant helps develop these new roles by "walking the talk" and then
helping clients learn from this new behavior. Consultants must consciously
use their own experiences as learning resources. They must bring to the
surface and discuss the dilemmas they face, clarify and share the reasoning
behind what they do and the choice points they face, and examine the
mistakes they have made. These tasks require a departure from the typical
role of consultant as content expert. He or she becomes a process expert
in learning how to learn and invites the participation of clients and
colleagues in that venture.

Consulting Dilemmas. As consultants, we hope to create a relationship with our clients that is characterized by free and informed consent.
Yet, when the service is an experiential learning process in which outcomes
are open-ended and the personal and interpersonal "ante" is to some extent
dependent on group interaction, this condition is difficult to create. Add
to this the propensities of organizations to "buy" products over processes,
defined objectives or outcomes over skills, short-term results with financial payoffs over longer-term development of people, and the problem of
creating a fair contract becomes clear.

Consultants help organizations frame action taking as a process of
changing both the situation and the shared meanings of those within the
situation, rather than as a product or outcome. This framework has several
implications. Foremost, processes are harder to understand and their
benefits less easy to grasp. Consultants must explain processes in terms of

products without putting themselves in a compromising position in terms of what will be delivered. While general outcomes can be described, precise changes in knowledge, skills, and attitudes cannot be predicted. Moreover, outcomes are often unsettling because empowered participants challenge old norms and ways of doing business. The fact that action technologies lead to organizational change may be construed positively in the planning stage, but it is almost always construed negatively by the managers who are eventually challenged by action groups. Processes also require a long-range view in a business world oriented toward quick, short-term results. People also learn to transform their perspective from that of an individual or department to that of the greater organizational good.

Four dilemmas grow out of this situation. First, it is difficult for the consultant to contract fairly when one party (the consultant) has a clear idea about what will happen experientially and little ability to predict or control the outcomes of the process, and the other party (the client) has little idea about what the process will be like and a strong need to control the outcomes. It is hard to predict how long the process will take because it depends on the willingness and ability of individuals to learn and the readiness of the organization to accept critical thinkers.

We have found it necessary to engage organizations in overview sessions, in which they get a taste of what is to come, and then to contract with them for a minimum of four months with sessions of two to four hours per week in small action-reflection learning groups. In this way, those who will make the decision to become involved have at least an initial experience with the process and also commit to a long enough period of time to ensure that the experience will begin to take root.

A second dilemma relates to the access to power of the action-reflection learning team. On the one hand, if the team has no authority to act, it cannot hope to change anything. On the other hand, if the team is going to make a difference, it is likely to challenge the status quo, question authority, and bring previously taboo issues to the surface. These approaches demand a high level of protection by management, though not necessarily involvement by management. Moreover, management may be perceived as the problem. By giving the team appropriate access to top management through written and verbal sanction and authority, by routinely reporting findings, and by learning to critically inquire about management's reasoning when differences of opinion exist, the team learns to work with its own and others' power. Unfortunately, we have seen many action teams quashed because of their inability either to secure sufficient authority to act or, once secured, to use their authority.

So much of the most powerful learning in action teams is serendipitous. This creates a third dilemma for consultants. Organizations value predictable results and are highly unlikely to even acknowledge results that were not part of the original game plans. There is a strong drift toward producing "something" for the organization, which can undermine the something that is being produced by the process. Often, that process-derived something threatens the status quo.

Finally, we agree with those who have argued that too often action research is more research than action or more action than research. It is extraordinarily difficult to aptly serve these two masters. With Argyris (1993), we believe that the goal of action research and action-reflection learning teams must be to produce actionable knowledge. Unfortunately, this knowledge is also likely to be fairly idiosyncratic and organizationally specific and therefore less generalizable.

Conclusion

To begin to build learning organizations through action technologies, consultants need a sense of the first steps. The use of action technologies entails, first, a clear understanding of the nature of the learning organization and how it differs from the current state of the client organization. One way of understanding this difference is to think in terms of frames.

Deal (1992) has described four frames, or lenses, through which individuals may lead organizations: factory, family, jungle, and cathedral. These frames are the mental models that predominate in organizations. The most common model among profit-oriented organizations is the factory. With this lens, the leaders focus on goals, roles, and tasks and create structures, processes, and changes that support these. Nonprofit organizations are more likely to embrace the family metaphor and emphasize the human resources of the organizations and quality-of-work-life issues. The organization as jungle emphasizes power, conflict, and negotiation. And the cathedral lens calls for charismatic leaders who can articulate a vision and align the organization around it.

Of course, effective organizations are led in all four areas. We think that the learning organization model asks organizations to restructure through a fifth lens—that of steward (Senge, 1990). In this lens, the organization drives toward continuous improvement. This means that it has an enhanced system for defining where it is currently against where it would like to be, for learning how to get where it wants to go, and for changing itself to make this journey possible. Viewed through such a lens, an organization would build systems for assessing current capacities for and barriers to change and learning, audit what its people know and help them plan careers that will lead them toward developing the roles they will need to fill in the future, enhance the change abilities of all employees, and create supportive informational infrastructures to disseminate and record what is learned.

Change is a cyclical process of creating knowledge (the change or innovation), disseminating it, implementing the change or knowledge, and institutionalizing what is learned (making it part of the organization's routines: operating procedure, policy, structure, and so on). In the learning organization, this process is facilitated by structures and consciously managed. The learning of individuals that is involved in making these changes is acknowledged and provided.

How then might the organization begin this process? It can begin by viewing itself through the learning lens, thinking about what it currently does that fits with this lens, and making plans to change what it currently does that prevents learning. We think that this process proceeds best with an action-reflection learning approach, which helps an organization change its mental model to one that promotes learning. Then, the tasks that might be undertaken to build a learning organization become clear to individuals and teams, and the work of building a learning organization continues, one step at a time. Facilitation of this process is the role of the adult education consultant.

References

Argyris, C. *Knowledge for Action: A Guide to Overcoming Barriers to Organizational Change.* San Francisco: Jossey-Bass, 1993.

Argyris, C., and Schön, D. A. *Theory in Practice: Increasing Professional Effectiveness.* San Francisco: Jossey-Bass, 1974.

Argyris, C., and Schön, D. A. *Organizational Learning: A Theory of Action Perspective.* San Francisco: Jossey-Bass, 1978.

Case, J. "The Change Masters." *Inc.,* Mar. 1992, pp. 58–70.

Deal, T. E. "Culture and Change." Lecture presented at the University of Texas, Austin, November 1992.

Honold, L. "The Power of Learning at Johnsonville Foods." *Training,* 1991, 4, 55–58.

Marsick, V. J., Cederholm, L., Turner, E., and Pearson, T. "Action Reflection Learning." *Training and Development,* 1992, 48 (8), 63–66.

Marsick, V. J., and Watkins, K. E. *Informal and Incidental Learning in the Workplace.* New York: Routledge & Kegan Paul, 1990.

Mezirow, J. *Transformative Dimensions of Adult Learning.* San Francisco: Jossey-Bass, 1991.

Revans, R. *Action Learning: New Techniques for Management.* London: Blond & Briggs, 1980.

Savage, C. M. *Fifth-Generation Management: Integrating Enterprises Through Human Networking.* Bedford, Mass.: Digital Press, 1990.

Senge, P. M. *The Fifth Discipline: The Art and Practice of the Learning Organization.* New York: Doubleday, 1990.

Watkins, K. E., and Marsick, V. J. *Sculpting the Learning Organization.* San Francisco: Jossey-Bass, in press.

KAREN E. WATKINS *is associate professor and program director of adult education and human resources development leadership, Department of Educational Administration, University of Texas, Austin.*

VICTORIA J. MARSICK *is professor and program director of adult education, Department of Adult and Higher Education, Teachers College, Columbia University.*

*The nature of adult education consulting work fosters practices that
are not only rich in options, rewards, and promises but also
personally and professionally reinvigorating.*

The Adult Educator as Consultant: Options, Rewards, and Promises

Sally Vernon, Lois J. Zachary

This volume mirrors the variety of practice settings, environments, and
cultures in which adult education consultants work. Through individualized reflections on practice, the contributing authors bring home the
reality of consulting as a viable practice option and career path for adult
educators.

The authors illustrate the multiple settings and situations, multiple
pathways, and multiple styles in which they practice. No two authors have
followed the exact same road and yet each is a successful consultant.
Multiple styles are revealed in the ways in which the authors describe the
products, philosophies, and processes that underlie their practices. Paral-
leling the diversity is the authenticity and idiosyncrasy of practice, the
hallmarks of these successful consultancies.

Most of the authors have worked as adult education consultants for a
long time. Several years ago, Ronald Gross (1989) characterized his own
consulting career path as "the way of the ronin":

> Ronin means literally, wave people—men and women who ride the
> waves of change on their own. . . . What constitutes this "way"? . . .
> Ronin need a repertoire of basic skills honed to a high level, including
> self-management, quick-study, speaking and writing, team-playing and
> team-building. . . . Doing ronin offers the maximum in self determina-
> tion, diversity and opportunity for initiative.

Our contributing authors are ronin. Until recently, adult education consulting was not as highly valued as the "specialized" services and products

offered by consultants from other disciplines. Given the reality of the learning society, the adult educator is now the resource of choice.

The important themes of these chapters are the degree to which people enjoy their day-to-day work and the energy that they derive from it. Webb's research and the other authors' testimonies here concur. The key to adult educators' career satisfaction as consultants resides in their understanding of who they are and what the consulting role means for them. The many answers to the question "What do I do for a living?" (Zachary, Moller) characterize this professional work as varied, multifaceted, and amorphous.

The authors of this volume recognize the complexity of the worlds in which they practice (Vernon, Watkins and Marsick). *Shifting paradigms*—for individuals, organizations, or communities—is a common phrase. One such shift concerns the ambiguity and importance of product versus process. Most of the authors here describe themselves as process experts. Yet each of them is only too aware that their clients are buying products over process (Vernon, Zachary, Watkins and Marsick). Brookfield makes the point that content is as important as process. Perhaps the balancing of content and process is the essence of successful consulting.

Flexibility also defines who the consultant is and what the consultant does (Webb). Flexibility has several dimensions, among them temporal flexibility, having to do with the use of time, and role flexibility, having to do with how the consulting process gets carried out.

The importance of understanding, building, nurturing, and sustaining interpersonal relationships is a common theme throughout these chapters as well, not only with respect to relationships among individuals within a client group (Brookfield, Moller) but also with respect to consultant-client and consultant-consultant relationships (Vericker). Indeed, Thomas is quick to advise that sharing and learning among colleagues is a professionally invaluable dynamic. Vericker extends our idea of relationships with the targeted use of technology and automation.

The actual consulting work performed by the authors is described as a series of processes involving common elements. For example, listening to the "voices" of clients frames the heart of most adult education practice (Brookfield, Goldberg). The notion of creating a learning community through group interaction is examined in terms of "groupthink" (Brookfield, Thomas), a reflection process that is essential in moving groups beyond the boundaries of their present thinking. Collaborative and collective learning speeds the transformation process (Friedman, Moller, Marsick and Watkins).

Walking the Talk

Perhaps the most prominent theme in this volume is the consultant as role model. Webb makes the point that we "need to grow ourselves as learners." Thomas talks about the value of the mentoring process as a way of learning from colleagues. Watkins and Marsick emphasize the point that consultant modeling of the learning process as individuals furthers the development of the learning organization. Howe's characterization of the consultant as the ultimate test of self-direction is certainly accurate.

Many of the authors here describe some of the negative aspects, such as frustration, that are a part of the consulting package (Brookfield, Vernon, Zachary, Thomas). It takes time to nurture connections (Howe, Vericker). It takes energy to remain self-directed (Brookfield, Webb, Howe, Friedman). It takes character to continuously place oneself in new situations and cultures. It takes courage to enter organizational cultures in times of rapid and continuous change (Vernon). Finally, it requires great risk-taking ability to not have a steady stream of income (Vericker, Thomas).

Joy of Practice

Despite these drawbacks of a consulting practice, it is clear that job satisfaction is high among the contributing authors. They express their joy in the generative nature of the work and exhilaration in practices that force praxis, for the consultant and for the client. In reflecting on their practices, the authors reveal how they have evolved as consultants, how they learn from their experiences, the respect each has for the client, and the care taken to ensure that the client is ready to learn.

Reinvigorating Self and Practice

Having completed her chapter, Gayle Moller wrote to us, "Thank you for forcing me to reflect on my practice. I need to do more of this." Her words capture what each of us has felt. The work of adult education consultants fosters continuous personal and professional reinvigoration.

The Adult Educator as Consultant describes many ways in which adult educators function as consultants, and the options, rewards, and promises of the work. Clearly, adult education consulting is not only a viable professional choice but a *desirable* one as well.

Reference

Gross, R. "Way of the Ronin: Work as Adventure." *Adult and Continuing Education Today,* 1989, *19* (22), 1.

SALLY VERNON is faculty chair and program director of the Department of Adult and Continuing Education, National-Louis University, Chicago, and is president of her own adult learning consulting firm.

LOIS J. ZACHARY is an education consultant with a private consulting practice in Fayetteville, New York.

APPENDIX:
TREASURY OF TIPS, TRAPS, AND TIDBITS

This treasury of bits and pieces of collected wisdom from the contributing authors outlines the *tips* (what works), *traps* (what to avoid), and *tidbits* (learnings) that are essential to a successful adult education consulting practice.

Tips	Traps	Tidbits
Give pro bono presentations and speeches.	Giving too much away.	Pro bono work is a source of exposure and potential business.
Have a separate business line with an answering machine.	Being penny wise and pound foolish.	Use technology to cost-effectively establish and maintain a professional image.
Never stop expanding your product line.	Losing sight of the changing marketplace because of daily pressure to get out the work.	Stay current and update and expand your product line.
Always ask for ongoing feedback from your clients.	Taking your competence, your learners, and your products for granted.	By using client feedback, you continually improve your product and better meet client needs.
Informal communication is sometimes more effective than formal communication.	Thinking that your clients have to be friends.	Building and nurturing relationships with clients is the key to successful consulting.
Never challenge your clients without providing adequate support.	Under- or overestimating your client and forgetting that your client is an adult learner.	Know your client well enough to propose appropriate and doable strategies.
Do not be afraid to share your own experiences with your clients.	Sharing too much and too often can result in lack of credibility with the client.	Authenticity is essential if you are to be credible and enhance your client's potential for learning.
Always clarify your role and responsibilities with your client up front.	Confusion in, confusion out. Your client will never be satisfied unless you have a mutual understanding of your roles and responsibilities.	Use a written agreement to negotiate and renegotiate your and your clients' roles and responsibilities.

NEW DIRECTIONS FOR ADULT AND CONTINUING EDUCATION, no. 58, Summer 1993 © Jossey-Bass Publishers

Tips	Traps	Tidbits
Find a collaborator or a mentor.	Being so afraid of the competition that you miss opportunities for collegial learning and professional growth.	Choose wisely, not on the basis of convenience.
Be visible.	Forgetting that 20 percent of a consultant's time is spent marketing, and that marketing encompasses a person and a product.	Make sure that you use multiple vehicles to continually convey to your publics who you are and what you do. You must market continually even if you are busy.
Each situation is a new and unique encounter.	Stepping on cultural toes and shutting down the learning process.	Do not forget that as a consultant you are always walking into someone else's culture. Never assume!!!
Do not put off until tomorrow what you can do today.	Time has a way of disappearing when you do not manage it properly.	Schedule and prioritize activities to include a balance of what you have to do, want to do, and should do.
Remember the "three p's" of consulting are people, process, and product. Of these, the priority is people.	Focusing too much on the product.	Know that it is the relationship that drives the process *and* the product.
Know and no your client.	You can easily get derailed and overwhelmed.	Set limits. Do your homework in advance.
Always consider the costs and benefits of doing business with new clients.	By considering only financial costs and benefits, you lose time, job satisfaction, and return business.	Make the time to do a cost-benefit analysis before signing the contract. Remember that cost is more than dollars and cents.
Ask yourself regularly what you are learning.	Becoming complacent and mentally lazy.	Consulting is synonymous with being habitually current.
Remember each contact is a potential customer.	Ignoring opportunities that are staring you in the face.	Take advantage of every opportunity to say who you are and what you do, even in the most familiar situations.
Choose your resources wisely.	Having a library that looks impressive but is never used.	Libraries are wonderful sources of current and useful information.

Tips	Traps	Tidbits
Keep your priorities straight.	Not doing what you really want to do.	Make the time to reflect on your practice.
Take good care of yourself.	Not being able to enjoy what you are doing.	If you cannot take care of yourself, you cannot take care of anybody else or your business.
Work is not everything.	Losing sight of the forest for the trees.	Make time to nurture yourself and restore balance in your life.

INDEX

ORDERING INFORMATION

NEW DIRECTIONS FOR ADULT AND CONTINUING EDUCATION is a series of paperback books that explores issues of common interest to instructors, administrators, counselors, and policy makers in a broad range of adult and continuing education settings—such as colleges and universities, extension programs, businesses, the military, prisons, libraries, and museums. Books in the series are published quarterly in spring, summer, fall, and winter and are available for purchase by subscription and individually.

SUBSCRIPTIONS for 1993 cost $45.00 for individuals (a savings of 20 percent over single-copy prices) and $60.00 for institutions, agencies, and libraries. Please do not send institutional checks for personal subscriptions. Standing orders are accepted.

SINGLE COPIES cost $14.95 when payment accompanies order. (California, New Jersey, New York, and Washington, D.C., residents please include appropriate sales tax.) Billed orders will be charged postage and handling.

DISCOUNTS FOR QUANTITY ORDERS are available. Please write to the address below for information.

ALL ORDERS must include either the name of an individual or an official purchase order number. Please submit your order as follows:
    Subscriptions: specify series and year subscription is to begin
    Single copies: include individual title code (such as CE1)

MAIL ALL ORDERS TO:
    Jossey-Bass Publishers
    350 Sansome Street
    San Francisco, California 94104

FOR SINGLE-COPY SALES OUTSIDE OF THE UNITED STATES CONTACT:
    Maxwell Macmillan International Publishing Group
    866 Third Avenue
    New York, New York 10022

FOR SUBSCRIPTION SALES OUTSIDE OF THE UNITED STATES, contact any international subscription agency or Jossey-Bass directly.